# In Pursuit of The Big Horse

## LEE PHILLIP FORMAN

TAYLOR ROAD PUBLICATIONS INC.

Published by Taylor Road Publications Inc.
180 N. LaSalle, Chicago, IL 60601

Designed by DePinto Graphic Design
Manufactured in the United States of America
Registered with the Library of Congress

ISBN: 0-9647339-2-7

Written for the women in my life; my wonderful mother Ida who nurtured me, my supportive wife Paula who inspired me, my loving daughter Melissa who encouraged me and my dear friend Rosemary and others like her who taught me courage by example in their fight against A.L.S.

# IN PURSUIT OF
# "THE BIG HORSE"

Sooner or later we all get to the same point in our lives. Our jobs seem to be only the mundane repetition of obligations; events are related to in terms of "it just doesn't seem that long ago." Days turn into months and the spiral of the clock turns months into the passage of time and middle age. We panic, desperate to do things before it becomes too late.

I have worked very hard to get where I am today but I am not complaining. I have a profitable law practice, a successful marriage of nearly thirty years, two employed and educated children and a cat that has used up 12 of her 9 lives. However, each of us has the need to feel that when it is all over, we have accomplished something that will be remembered, or at least recorded, forever. How does a 51-year old, so far a non-entity, where eternity is concerned, become part of history by design?

I have explored all the possibilities, including attempting to catch 200 dimes loaded up on each of my elbows at the same time; bouncing a basketball for two weeks straight, and drinking a fresh milkshake through a straw in under a minute. Those and a thousand other gags are not befitting my station in life or my somatotype. Besides, I don't relish the thought of my entire existence being justified in terms of the ability to perform an act which has no socially redeeming value.

I found myself, more and more, visiting our local racetracks and off track betting parlors and becoming mesmerized by the challenge of picking a winner. These small victories seemed to insulate me from the drudgeries of my profession and also provided an escape for me, and most of my available capital. Then one day it happened.

One day in late summer 1991 when visiting Chicago's Arlington International Racecourse, I pictured myself in the winner's circle after a major stakes race, taking a photo with my own horse. I imagined patting my steed on the nose and congratulating him on the win, and I could almost feel the weight of the crystal trophy as I held it high into the sun for a photograph. A rush of adrenaline ran through my body as the excitement of the imagined moment faded. The seed was sown. The quest for such a horse and such a photograph would be my goal.

I have been told that only once, and only if he is truly lucky, will a horseman ever be blessed with a Thoroughbred swift enough to chase the legends of the past. At the track, I am told, such a horse isn't often called by his name. He is simply known as "the big horse." On the day of a big race a groom is apt to call out, "everybody out of the way…big hoss comin' out." A gaggle of reporters and TV cameras follow the horse, its trainer and its owner. I would be such an owner.

This book documents my quest to make my dream come true. I dedicate my efforts to all of those who dream.

—Lee Forman

*"If a little knowledge is dangerous*
*then a lot of knowledge is much too unsafe to use."*

CHAPTER **1**

# GAINING AN
# EDUCATION

As I looked around Hawthorne Race Course, I could not believe that over three years had passed since I first set out in my quest for "the big horse." It was now the day before Thanksgiving in 1994 and my wife Paula and I nervously walked into the paddock area just before the Illinois Cavalier Stakes Race. The photos on the wall, the food concession stands, the shoe shine chair and the tellers behind the betting cages were all now familiar sights. All sorts of people greeted us on our way to see our newly-purchased 2 year-old gelding Booker, off in search of a second major stakes victory and possibly a championship. Waves, slaps on the back, salutes and all possible forms of good luck signals formed a pathway as we proceeded through the crowd of familiar faces. I felt like a president or a king greeting his subjects as we parted from the crowd and proceeded down the stairs where the unmistakable smell of the paddock area met us.

In a very few moments, Booker would load into the starting gate, and would attempt to defeat some of the best 2 year-olds in the midwest. The odds makers had him the best bet of the day and the bettors had him on the tote board at 3-5, with his next closest competitor at 9-1. If he could win this race, there is no doubt in my mind that he would be voted "Champion Illinois Two-Year Old Colt or Gelding of 1994" and possibly the state's "horse of the year." That photograph and that trophy presentation would fulfill a quest that had started with only a vision and which now might actually come true.

I was actually shaking as I watched jockey E.T. Baird get a leg up from Pat Devereaux, our assistant trainer, and lead Booker toward the starting gate. My adrenaline was flowing and I knew that everything was on the line. The newspapers had carried a story headlined: "will dreams be fulfilled or hearts broken?"

My grip on Paula's hand tightened as I watched Booker loaded into the number 2 post position. We turned and looked at each other. Paula touched my cheek and smiled in a reassuring way and then apologized as she turned away and did not look as the race started. Paula had never watched a race, out of nervousness or maybe superstition. She always looked away and listened to my yells and screams to determine just how well or how poorly our horse was doing in a race. All I could reflect on now was how this quest started, and all the fun and heartbreak we'd experienced along the way. I closed my eyes and thought back.

It was early August, 1991. I had found a notice in the racetrack's racing program that the Illinois Thoroughbred Breeders and Owners Foundation would be holding a seminar at Arlington Park the next Sunday for anyone interested in learning about owning or breeding racehorses. This seemed to be an intelligent place to start my quest. I called and registered my wife and I for Sunday August 11, 1991. The cost was $75 per person and included a lunch after the lecture and free admission to the park. The worst thing that could happen is that I might lose a few hundred bucks at the track, which had already become a common occurrence.

Paula and I arrived at Arlington Park Race Track about 7:30 a.m. for the lecture. We had no idea what type of people we would meet or what the program would consist of. Upon driving up to our assigned meeting area we were happy to find that the other 25 or so attendees appeared, at first glance, to be people of some substance coming from similar walks of life.

We were gathered up and taken by a small bus to the barn area of Arlington. During the ride the group kept somewhat to themselves and conversation was minimal.

Our first stop was the barn of Neil and Michelle Boyce, trainers working as a husband and wife team. The purpose of this visit was to see first-hand what a barn looks like and how it operates. Even though their barn was immaculate, you could sense that to be in this game, you must immediately get used to a certain odor that one would usually only encounter on days that a landscaper fertilized his lawn or your dog Fluffy got sick.

Michelle explained that the horses are fed twice a day and she described the type of diet the animals are put on and the cost of the same. For the most part, the racehorse is fed a hot mash composed of grains and chemicals that are designed for the individual horse's needs. Hay bales are left hanging on the sides of the stalls and the horse has a bucket of water which is kept filled. Those delicacies could run $5 to $8 a day, depending on the number of horses being fed. On average, the stalls are about 15 feet square, and soft straw is constantly changed as a flooring. The animals do what they have to in the straw and you are reminded constantly to look where you are stepping when entering a stall.

The Thoroughbred is a nervous animal. Although I am a rider, the animals we've seen to this point seem to be wild and incapable of love and affection. We attempted a few times to pet the horses in the Boyces' barn but did so with some reservation. I was hoping that this was not a normal reaction of the Thoroughbred horse because I would be very disappointed if I could not show some love and affection to the animals we would eventually own.

Outside the barn we stood in a semicircle while a handsome gelding was led in by trainer and ex-rider Gerard McGrath. He explained the anatomy of the horse, which first introduced us to such terms as hocks, cannon bones, and fetlocks.

The most interesting fact we learned is that the part of the horse that makes it run fast is the only part you cannot examine or measure. It is what horsemen call "heart." Like the song, "You gotta have heart"; in racing, the will to win is what separates horses which earn millions from horses which end up pulling milk wagons. Some trainers swear that they can look into the eyes of a horse and tell if a horse has heart.

McGrath explained that a good trainer can watch a horse jog and tell quite a bit about his ability. Have you ever watched a jock walk down the street on a college campus? Could you pick him out over the local chess champion or the fat kid who always gets picked last in the choose-up games?

For novices, McGrath left us with a fair understanding of what we would be looking for in an animal. Generally one that is alert and athletic-looking. The horse should have a confident gait which is efficient and wastes no motion. The color of a horse has no relationship to its ability to run although there seems to be a premium on gray horses if they meet all the other standards.

We were then taken to the business office of the track. We met with the racing steward and his assistants who explained how races are made up. I could never before imagine the mechanics that went into making up a racing program.

The sport of racing is no different than any other promotion: you produce something that people will pay to see. The owner of the track guarantees and puts up the purses, and, in most races, owners pay no entry fee.

The purse money comes back to the track owner out of a percentage of the mutual handle on the race. If the crowd is betting big enough, the track owner makes back his purse plus a percentage allowed him by state law for producing the race. The remainder of the take-out is paid to the government in taxes and to various horsemen's associations. The balance of the money bet over and above the take-out is distributed to the people who placed and won their bets. In pari-mutuel betting, the track returns from 72 to 85% of the money bet back to the public.

We learned that in almost every race, the winning owner gets 60% of the purse, second place gets 20%, third 11%, forth 6% and fifth 3% of the purse.

Some races carry money added to the purse by associations that sponsor the race such as the well known

Breeders' Cup or by state breeding associations, that make the extra purse only available to horses which have been foaled in that state.

If you breed a quality mare with a stallion that has been registered with Breeders' Cup, the weanling can be registered as a Breeders' Cup candidate upon the payment of $500 by the owner. All of that money is collected and distributed during the year in various Breeders' Cup races, culminating with a seven race Breeders' Cup Day program worth ten million dollars. The winner of the Breeders' Cup Classic can win 60% of $3,000,000. That should be enough incentive for anyone.

I was surprised at how small the racing office at Arlington was in correlation to all that is accomplished there. We were introduced to Richard L. Duchossois, Chairman of the Board of Arlington International Racecourse and also the man responsible for rebuilding the park after it burned down. It is rumored that he will never be able to recoup the millions he invested into the business. Since rebuilding Arlington, Mr. Duchossois has been able to capture two coveted Eclipse Awards and induction into the HPBA Hall Of Fame. The man himself is impressive. With all his financial accomplishments, you would expect a stuffy, executive type. Instead, you are greeted by a humble and sincere person.

Next, we met the recently-hired general manager. He explained the operations of the racing office.

Every 13 days a book is published which lists the races proposed. The trainers enter their horses into races that match their abilities. Entries close two days before the race date at exactly 1 p.m. Each day's list contains at least nine different kinds of races and four or five alternatives. If a race is not filled up by a minimum number of acceptable entries, it is the job of the racing secretary to fill the race or select a race from those races posted by trainers. This is referred to as putting up a race, which means that if a trainer cannot find a race for a horse, then he may suggest a type of race and post it on a board. The other trainers may enter their horses in the posted race hoping that it will take place.

Many of us were confused as to how parity is maintained in the races and why someone could not enter an exceptionally fast horse in a race with slower horses to ensure a win. This is where conditions and claiming prices come into play. A horse who is very young or has never run is generally entered into a maiden special weight race. This is an open race that does not handicap horses by weight. All horses carry the same weight. The weight a horse carries consists of the total weight of the jockey and the saddle plus extra weights if needed. After a race, you will always notice that the jockey removes the saddle and holds it while he or she weighs in.

There are other races that handicap certain horses by asking them to carry more weight than other horses in order to even up their abilities. It is similar to the handicap system used in golf where some golfers are awarded additional strokes while golfing a superior opponent. A horse that wins a maiden race will be ineligible to run again in such a condition. He is then eligible to run in any open race. Preference in some races is given to the horses that have won the most money. Horses that win races will seek to improve the quality of their competition and elevate their status by entering into races with larger purses. Merely entering a horse into a race does not always ensure that the horse will run in that race. In some races horses are classified by weights; the more they have won and the better fields they have beaten, the higher their respective weights will be. Where some 50 horses enter a specific race, preference is shown to the higher weights.

Therefore, on its way to the top, a horse must earn its entry into some races unless the owners choose to buy their way into the race. In the Breeders' Cup Classic, a buy-in (paying a supplementary fee to enter a horse that has not been nominated for the race) will cost the owners $360,000.

There are a variety of conditioned races which may be entered based upon the money the horse has won, the number of races it has won, the time since it last won a race, and the horse's age. It is interesting to note that all horses have their birthdays on January 1st. They all turn one year older on the same day regardless of their actual birthdays.

For the horse that keeps on winning, sooner or later it will run out of readily available conditions. For such a horse, handicap or stakes races, are available. The very best races (about 5 percent of all stakes run) are graded from the most impressive Grade 1 down to the least impressive Grade 3. It should be noted that the winning of a Graded stakes race is both a financially and professionally rewarding event.

Most novices think the Kentucky Derby is the most prestigious Grade 1 event in racing. They are far from correct. All Derbys, including the Kentucky Derby, are limited to 3-year olds and horses do not usually reach their full potential until their fourth year of life and beyond. First prize in the derby is only $300,000 as compared to

$600,000 in the grade 1 Arlington Million or $1,800,000 in the Breeders' Cup Classic.

Not everyone can run in a Derby. Some Derbies have committees that select the field from nominees to ensure an interesting race. It has been said, and just as often disputed, that if there is any unfairness in the sport it is at this level where jealousy, bias and prejudice may at times appear.

Those who choose to run their two and three-year-olds in these events are generally doing so not only to win the prize money but to establish the abilities of the horse to stand at stud. Most of these prize winners never see racing in their fifth year because they go on to stud services at anywhere from $5,000 to $200,000 per live foal.

With the ability of a stud to breed once a week or better, many prize derby winners are pulled from the dangers of the track and the owners retire on the annuity of the value of their horse's stud service.

For the horses that are capable of competing at an open level, there are a variety of stakes and handicap races all over the country and in Europe and Canada. It is quite a game for owners and trainers, traveling across this land with a well-bred winner trying to dodge those horses that can beat you and enter the softer races with rich pots that have little or no competition. The ability to pick the right race is one that few trainers have and transcends the ability of the trainer to get the horse in condition for the race. A few trainers in the business have both and they always seem to be on top. Distance and track conditions are two factors that change to maintain parity. Races are run over distances from 2 furlongs to 2 miles. The track surface can vary from dirt to grass and from fast to slow depending on the hardness of the surface. The moisture content of the track can change its condition from fast to sloppy or muddy. Owners and trainers need to be familiar with a horse's ability in all conditions and anticipate whether the race will be run in a condition most favorable to or unfavorable to the horse.

Our group was mesmerized by the volume of information cast in our direction. The sum and substance of the lecture was to make us aware that the continuation of our education was a necessity. A member of our group asked what becomes of those horses that are unable to win a maiden race or compete on the higher levels? We were told that this is where the claiming system comes into effect.

Horses that cannot compete on the same level as allowance, handicap or stakes horses may enter races in which any horse in the race may be claimed (purchased) by any other owner. The claiming price is set before the race is run and claiming races in the U.S. are run for as high as $180,000 and as low as $1,000. At Arlington we rarely see a claiming race above $50,000 and never lower than $4,000. One can readily understand why a horse that has been winning stakes races where the prize may be over $60,000, is not going to be raced in an event where it can be purchased for $20,000 or $30,000.

The same holds true for a horse that can win at a level of $25,000. The owner is rarely going to take the chance of running against $5,000 claimers and subject his horse to being claimed. Whenever an open competition horse drops from the allowance ranks to the claiming ranks for the first time at an exceptionally low price level, the health of the horse or its abilities are always questioned by handicappers. Claiming races make up a majority of the races held in the United States.

The seminar group was then taken over to Arlington Trackside Restaurant for a lecture. Trackside was originally Ditka's Trackside until Arlington reopened after the fire and the Levy Corporation took over the food services for the Arlington International Co. They now operate the establishment as an off track betting parlor (OTB).

We were addressed first by Michael Frierdich, president of the Illinois Thoroughbred Breeders and Owners Foundation who, as a tax attorney, is considered an expert on IRS requirements on the racing of horses.

The most important aspect of the lecture was to distinguish the difference between horse racing as a hobby and as a business. The IRS treats deductions much differently for business purposes than for hobbies.

Racing and breeding is a business when the taxpayer conducts it as a business by keeping proper books and records and adopting methods to make a profit comparable to other businesses. The taxpayer must devote a substantial period of time to the activity and keep records of time spent. The owner must expect the value of the horses to appreciate and must show that he has had success in the activity or similar activities. He must have a history of gains rather than successive losses, and be able to show a reasonable amount of profit in order for the IRS to allow him to continue in the activity as a business as opposed to his keeping it open just to generate a loss. The fact that the owner derives an element of personal pleasure or recreation from racing is not sufficient for it to lose the status of a business.

Frierdich went on to tell us about passive loss limitations, at-risk limitations and what expenses are deductible in horse racing. The most salient fact I learned was that the cost of a two-year-old horse could be depreciated over four years and all other horses over eight years. Capital gains on an animal apply only after the animal is owned 24 months. Probably the most important thing I carried away from the lecture on taxes is the need for good record-keeping. I intend from this day forth to keep all my green sheets, program books, losing tickets, and entrance badges to prove my attendance when the little guy with the green eyeshade and specs comes to look over my books.

The last lecture was given by Michelle Boyce. Her purpose was to explain how and where to buy a horse. We were introduced to an auction catalog and we were taught how to read the pedigree pages to determine the value of the horse, or at least which horse might have the breeding to win. The sales catalogs are distributed when there is to be an auction of horses. Each horse is assigned a hip number, and a history of their breeding is given in the catalog.

The first bit of information we are drawn to is the sire of the horse. I am told that in Illinois at this time the sires that are producing the most winners are Zen, Spy Signal and Bob's Dusty. Those horses stand at stud for prices from $2,500 to $5,000. On the national level a horse such as Seattle Slew might bring as much as $200,000 for a live foal. After determining the ability of the sire, we are to examine the dams (mothers) for four generations. If all of the dams in the line have produced horses that have raced and won, we are looking at a strong bottom line on the dam's side.

We must determine if the seller of the foal is culling his herd. Some breeders keep the best of the stock and sell the rest. An otherwise flawless breeding can result in a crooked legged horse or an injured animal and this will not show up on paper. The novice is advised to stay clear of a farm which keeps some of its foals and sells some, without professional assistance. Those that are sold are more likely to have been culled due to defects.

To me the most enjoyable part of the lecture was the end when Michelle gave us the history of the Thoroughbred horse and the theory of breeding.

I learned that the idea of matching horses in a race to see which could run the fastest probably has existed about as long as men have owned horses. Inscribed tablets uncovered in Asia Minor indicate that Assyrian kings maintained stables of running and war horses as early as 1500 B.C. There was chariot racing at the Olympic Games in Greece in the seventh century B.C. and mounted races were run in Rome during the first century B.C. to the first century A.D.

Perhaps the first racing purse was 40 pounds of gold offered in England during the reign of Richard the Lion Hearted. The race was run over three miles with knights as riders.

The horses in the days of old carried over 450 pounds of armor and were bred for mass and strength out of the Arabian horse. With the advent of gun powder, knights in armor and lances passed, and with them the value of the stout horse. In its place the importance of breeding speed into the animal to outflank and outrun the enemy became of primary importance.

There were many small breeds of animals under 14 hands high, which existed then. However, they were incapable of bearing up under the grueling use. What was needed was a type roughly as tall as the heavy breeds but considerably lighter, with good bone, strong back and powerful muscle. A horse which could combine speed and stamina.

As early as the 16th century, a variety of horses— Arabs, Barbs and Turks—were brought to England for breeding. The value of the fastest studs increased as the animals proved themselves. With increasing numbers of horses boasting of speed to gain value, the need for trials of speed became more numerous and more interesting. There were racetracks laid out at Doncaster in 1595. Interestingly enough, Cromwell issued a proclamation in 1654 forbidding racing for six months apparently fearing that the racecourse might become a cavalier meeting place (or maybe he was just the first to foresee the creation of the B.D.H. broken down horseplayer).

Racing in those days was limited to matches between two horses that were decided in heats with the horses carrying heavy weights of 168 pounds (12 stone). There were no grandstands and the prizes were large by today's standards. Unfortunately, no one kept a stud book or a record of the breeding until well into the 18th Century.

Cuthbert Routh's stud book from 1718 to 1752 was one of the first. Almost all of the records kept in the days to follow were coveted.

The history of American Thoroughbred racing parallels that of the English. Horses were brought here as early as 1625 but with no record of bloodlines. There are records of racing on Long Island as far back as 1665. Early records show racing in the Carolinas in 1734, Maryland in 1745 and Virginia in 1734. All of these were presumably very informal affairs. Governor Ogle introduced racing between pedigreed horses, in the English style, at Annapolis in 1745. This date may be said to mark the beginning of Thoroughbred breeding and racing in North America.

The first Thoroughbred importation was the stallion Bully Rock in 1730. However, there were few mares of racing heritage to mate with; and being 21, there was little time. His connection to modern racehorses is almost nil.

The first continuous record of American racing begins with the American Turf Register and Sporting Magazine, published first in Baltimore in September 1829 by John Stuart Skinner, a good friend of Francis Scott Key, the author of "The Star Spangled Banner."

The *American Stud Book* began in 1873 and was purchased in 1896 by The Jockey Club, which still conducts all American registrations.

In America, all male lines go back to the sires: Herod, Matchem, and Eclipse. Most of the mares might well have sprung from completely non-Thoroughbred stock. The authenticity of the bloodlines of American mares was a point of contention between American and English breeders for years. They led to the passage in 1913 of the so-called Jersey Act which prohibited the registration of any Thoroughbred not traceable in every respect to the General Stud Book. The Jersey Act was rescinded in 1949 when it became apparent that many American-bred Thoroughbreds, banned from the general stud book, were outperforming their English bred rivals on the turf.

A horse's ancestry is known by the term "pedigree." The racing record of sons and daughters of the sire and dam are the most important measure of a horse's pedigree. The term family only represents the female side of the pedigree and a horse is not a half brother or sister unless it is from the same dam.

Certain sires have earned status as "Chef de Race" which entitles their progeny to certain points in a system of ranking pedigree. Strangely enough, some of our most famous racehorses have not been accorded such an honor for their failure to consistently produce winners. Secretariat, for one, is not a "Chef de Race." However, his father, Bold Ruler, his grandfather Nasrullah, and his great-grandfather Nearco were.

Having been guided through the history of the Thoroughbred I now felt a sense of belonging to history by becoming involved with the continuation of a sport that has its roots firmly planted in the evolution of man.

The last bit of educational material we received on this day covered the actual expenses I could expect to pay to become involved in the sport. To board a racehorse with a trainer at a track, ran from $40 to $60 per day. In addition, the trainer gets 10% of the winnings. The jockey gets either a percentage of the purse, in most cases 10%, or a flat fee of $50 to $100 per race.

When boarding on a farm, the cost runs from $5 to $30 per day and the actual training of a young horse, from $20 to $50 per day. Veterinarians are notorious for bills that can bring tears to an owner. A good horseshoer on track gets about $60 per horse.

On the positive side, the purse in a maiden race is about $18,000 at Arlington, with $11,220 to the winner. By comparison, an allowance race for non-winners of three, has a purse of about $26,400 with the winner receiving

$15,840.

One could purchase a 2-year old ready to run for as little as $10,000 and break even on the winning of its first maiden race. There is always the chance of buying the "one in a million horse" for as little as $2000 or $3000.

After the lecture ended, Paula and I retired to the Million Room for lunch and to interview some trainers for possible employment. The interviews were rather unproductive, as I liked everyone I met equally. Each trainer had individual outstanding qualities and the only thing I knew for certain that day was that I wanted in. My next task would be finding the right trainer.

*"Like trying to find a needle in a needle stack."*

CHAPTER **2**

# FINDING
# A TRAINER

If I was going into racing seriously, I would have to hire a trainer. I searched through the lecture material until I found a list of about 30 or so local trainers and their business phones. I leafed through the names trying to remember those I had met at the seminar.

I jotted down a few names of trainers I had seen win at the track and began to call them one at a time.

I made appointments with several trainers and visited their barns. In each case we exchanged information and small talk about the expenses involved in racing, my experience level, and their financial requirements. Prior to my exposure to all of this it would have been my opinion that trainers would be rather choosy as to which owners they would take on and that I might be rejected by some.

After several interviews it became readily apparent that an owner is just a pen and a checkbook and that anyone willing to part with the cost of a horse can hire any trainer in the business. Weighed down with that thought, I continued my search until I visited the barn of Ernie T. Poulos.

I met Ernie Poulos on August 25, 1991. I called first

and made an appointment to meet him at about 9:30 a.m.
I drove into Arlington and for the first time in my life drove
right up to the pass gate, to the barn area and proudly
announced that I was a guest of Mr. Ernie T. Poulos. The
guard called to Ernie's barn and in a few minutes I was on
my way to barn 28 which was located in the far southwest
corner of the track.

As I drove up to the barn, a large white late-model
Cadillac went past me driven by a strikingly-attractive woman
whom I would later learn was Dee Poulos, Ernie's wife.

I got out of my car in the middle of several horses
receiving baths, bales of hay flying in all directions and a
myriad of people scurrying around as if a war were being
prepared for. In the middle of all this confusion, Ernie sat in
this little six by six office strewn with Daily Racing Forms
and a variety of booklets and note pads.

Ernie was an imposing figure, about five foot eight
any way you looked at him. As he sat there, he encompassed
the chair which strained under his massive weight. Gray salt
and peppered, thinning hair, topped his weathered face.
Massive bags almost hid his steely eyes which briefly gave
me the once-over before he pronounced his initial greeting...
"sit." "So you wanna own fuckin' horses?..." "You'll lose
your fuckin' ass if you don't listen to what I say." I can't
remember what came out of my mouth after that, but I am
certain it was not what I normally would say under the cir-
cumstances. I must have sounded like a 10-year-old kid
meeting Babe Ruth for the first time. The only thing I can
remember now about that conversation is his asking me how
much money I would risk and that I probably would need a
partner. I remember mumbling something about $25,000

and agreeing to allow Ernie to find me a partner.

Within a short time I really got to know Mr. Ernie T. Poulos and his family, and I think that the following description of the man I chose as my trainer is important to the whole story. It will also be important to understand Ernie in order to understand some of the decisions we would make together.

Ernie was born around Taylor and Halsted in Chicago, only a hop, skip and a jump from Sportsman's and Hawthorne Park. Born to Greek parents, Ernie was first introduced to horses through his grandfather's horse and wagon enterprises. These were the bootleg days and for $2 his grandfather rented people a horse and wagon with 10 quarts of booze under the seat. The people took the whole rig and then went out and sold the booze.

By the time Ernie was six he was hanging around the stockyards where horse sales were a regular item. He told me that he used to sit on the rail as the horses came through and act as a shill. He would get $.50 a head for getting on and riding a horse so that the auctioneer could say it was "kid broke."

At age 12, little Ernie became interested in gaited horses, fine harness horses and hackney ponies. The urge for adventure motivated him to run off with the Clyde Beatty Circus. There he met Arthur Konyot who had "high school" horses and later trained dressage horses for Arthur Godfrey. Poulos's ambition was to be a lion-tamer, that is until he saw Clyde Beatty get mauled.

Ernie traveled the western states with the circus, hanging Clyde Beaty signs up on barns and tearing down the signs of their competitor, Cole Brothers.

Eventually, Poulos decided life on the road was not for him. He returned home and went back to school until adventure called again and he joined the Merchant Marine at age 16.

World events intervened and he found himself on the Normandy beachhead on D-Day. Ernie's post-war days included some semi-pro football and a short jaunt into the wholesale meats business. All along, he continued to have a love affair with horses.

Ernie married and had children. That marriage ended, but like all other Poulos stories, Ernie, like a cat, landed on his feet and married Dee, the love of his life and probably the best partner in the business he has ever had.

In 1968, Ernie added a couple of Thoroughbreds to his stable and began racing as an owner. Strange to relate, but he became disenchanted with trainers and took out his own license to train in Florida.

One of his first good horses was Gentleman Born and one of his first good clients was C.K. Hudson of Sundial Stables.

C.K. owned a fire extinguisher manufacturing company in Northbrook, Ill. Ernie went to work for C.K. caring for the horses that pulled C.K.'s fire wagon which was used as an advertisement. C.K. took young Ernie under his wing and led him into sales. Ernie always called C.K. the "old man" even though C.K. died very young.

C.K. had a fiery personality which was quite distinctive and all his own. He would tell Ernie that when he (C.K.) died he would return as a horse and that Ernie should look for him.

Two years after C.K.'s death, Ernie was at a sale at

Hialeah. Along came a little horse named Pokerhound. As the groom led the young horse past Ernie, the horse stopped and looked Ernie in the eye. The groom pulled the horse by the shank and led it away. Pokerhound turned, looked at Ernie, and pulled the shank out of the groom's hand. The groom gave the horse a smack and led it away again. Again, Pokerhound turned, looked at Ernie and yanked the shank away from the groom and returned to the shocked Poulos.

The horse had just sold for $1,800. Ernie, certain that this was C.K., immediately offered $2,000 for the horse. A deal was negotiated and $2,200 again united the friends Ernie and C.K. (now Pokerhound).

The horse went on to earn $160,000 and Ernie swears on a stack of bibles that the horse's fiery personality was the same as C.K.'s.

When Pokerhound's career as a racehorse ended, Ernie put him out to pasture and tore up his papers so that no one else could take advantage of the ownership of his friend. When Ernie tells this story to anyone other than to a good friend, people think he is a little loose.

Young Ernie had been an imposing figure. A handsome youth, with rippling muscles and wavy black hair. I saw a picture of him and he looked like a young Desi Arnaz. Now the rippling muscles have given way to tons of good Greek food and the once athletic body is now held up by a small wooden cane. The wavy black hair was gray and thin but the desire to be number one still propelled Ernie into a workday that puts him into the hospital once or twice a year to bring his sugar count back into triple digits.

Ernie has trained notable Thoroughbreds such as Bundle of Iron, Royal Proctor, Gentle Vixen, I'm Artie,

Barbery, Jazzburger, Brady Bay and Hi Oaks Silver. At the time of my first meeting with him, neither Ernie nor I knew that he was about to reach the pinnacle of his career in October of 1991.

Ernie had several owners in his barn, one of whom was Jeff Sullivan, owner of Sullivan Pontiac in Arlington Heights. Ernie and Jeff had, up to that point, a rather up-and-down success rate, losing six figures at first before coming up with a horse called Super Roberto which earned $168,302 for the pair.

Ernie was always on the lookout for a good buy and when a New York owner was willing to part with a 2-year old that had run second to Dixieland Brass for a mere $125,000, Ernie could not resist.

At first, Jeff could resist and offered only $100,000 for the horse. It was only after coaxing from Ernie that Jeff parted with the extra $25,000 over his budget and purchased Black Tie Affair.

Black Tie Affair was bred in Ireland by Stephen Peskoff and consigned to the Saratoga Yearling Sale where he was originally purchased for $85,000. The stallion was by the Mr. Prospector stallion Miswaki. The dam was Hat Tab Girl, a stakes winner of $94,681 by Al Hattab. Poulos and Sullivan purchased the horse from Hudson River Farm. The 2-year old had been trained by Walter Reese.

In the three years Poulos and Sullivan raced Black Tie Affair he won 18 races (13 stakes, 11 graded), placed second nine times, and third six times. In 1991, the 5-year old was on the board in 9 of 10 races winning his last 7 straight stakes; the last of which I witnessed in amazement from a bar in downstate Illinois during Father's Day at the U of I.

There in southern Illinois, hundreds of miles away from the running of the Breeders' Cup Classic race, I witnessed another person's dreams being realized as the big gray horse led wire to wire earning Jeff $1,800,000 in prize money.

I had selected a trainer and yeah, "I wanna own fuckin' horses."

*"Son, if you want to know what your bride will look like when she is fifty, look at her mother."*

CHAPTER **3**

# DEE AND COMPANY, INCLUDING TERI

When you hire a trainer you enter his entire world. People in the racing industry begin to know you only by the trainer you have selected. Everybody figures that birds of a feather flock together. Ernie, I have just found out, comes along with a whole entourage.

First, there is Ernie's wife, Dee. I do not feel I could do justice to this lovely woman by just describing her as tall and attractive. She has impeccable taste in western clothing and stands out in a crowd. A bright red cowgirl hat and matching boots are a compliment to the western jewelry which usually adorn her body abundantly.

Dee is a soft-spoken woman of few words. However, one is wise to stay on the good side of this tigress. Right off the bat when talking to Dee, I noticed that one sensitive subject was one of Ernie's ex-grooms, Teri. I am a good learner and quickly eliminated that name from my vocabulary when conversing with Dee.

During the first few days in my association with Ernie, I was required to apply for an owner's license and various passes and badges. Ernie does not have the patience for such details which he leaves up to Dee. She handles them with such ease that it certainly made me feel welcome.

I noticed that Dee also signed all the checks and handled most of the purveyors the stable did business with. She insulated Ernie from the daily stresses associated with running the business. Almost nothing upsets Dee, with the exception of the mention of Teri.

Charlie Bettis was Ernie's assistant trainer. Charlie was rather quiet but appeared to be competent. Charlie seemed to be in his early forties and was rather take-charge in nature. From what little I have observed these few days, there was a strain in the relationship between Charlie and Ernie.

Rocky Feminella is as interesting a character as you would care to meet. He appeared to be entering his eighties as he hobbled around the barn on his heels with short little steps, cleaning the tack and doing odd jobs. Rocky was a New Yorker who was raised in Brooklyn. He walked onto a track in New York with a top hat and a suitcase and begged the famous Hal Bishop for a job. Bishop, known as the "king of claiming," started Rocky out as a hot walker, then as a groom and assistant trainer. Rocky brags that he once led the famous Willie Shoemaker around a ring on a pony as a youngster. When Bishop moved to Illinois he shared a barn with Ernie and when Hal retired, Rocky moved over to the Poulos stables.

Rocky has a deathly fear of flying and travel and spends his entire existence on the backstretch. Like Ernie, he found himself on Omaha Beach on D-Day and was recently recognized as one of the 50-year survivors of that conflict. Rocky is the type of nuts and bolts employee who keeps Poulos stables together.

The rest of Ernie's staff consisted of grooms and hot walkers, all of whom referred to Ernie as "the boss." I felt that Ernie had surrounded himself with a team of competent people, and they all seemed to work well with Ernie in the driver's seat.

A few days later Dee called me to meet Ernie at Arlington Park. I was to bring a check for $100 and at least the same in cash. I was going to apply for my license to own racehorses and open an account with the horseman's book-keeper.

When I met Ernie at the racing office he was in quite a hurry. He rushed me through the licensing procedures. I was impressed by the way the Arlington staff allowed Ernie the liberties in cutting corners in normal procedures. After I was fingerprinted, photographed and had opened my account with the horseman's bookkeeper, I was rushed out of the office by Ernie.

He explained that he was late and wanted to meet with a lawyer that afternoon. I told him that he was in luck since I might be able to help him. We sat down to talk business.

Ernie said that he felt a duty to care for his people and that one of his ex-grooms, Teri Madrid, who owned a farm in Harvard, Illinois, was about to lose the farm to an unscrupulous businessman who had cheated her. He went on to tell me that her daughter had been having nightmares since she and her mother found a finger in a bag of french fries that they had purchased at a local fast food chain. He also told me that this woman was dying of cancer of the pancreas which went undiagnosed as a result of the negligence of a doctor and that he was going to find an attorney to help her with all of these problems.

My immediate reaction was that I had hit a vein of pure gold. This gal sounded like a walking law practice. I agreed to meet her and help Ernie out.

Paula and I took a ride out to Harvard, Illinois, to meet Teri. When we arrived we were greeted by the largest, blackest dog I had ever seen. The dog jumped up and started licking the windshield of my small Mercedes convertible. Two small children corralled the dogs and escorted Paula and I into the house.

The farm appeared to be about 20 acres with a large barn and an indoor arena, a few out-buildings, three or more small corrals and a ranch-styled farmhouse into which we were led.

Once inside. we walked into a dark living room that smelled of death. There on the couch, under a blanket, watching TV, was Teri.

She weakly asked us to come in, sit down, and excused herself for not getting up or offering us a drink. Paula opted to take the children outside and visit with the animals while I proceeded to take an information sheet on her various legal problems. I took about two hours of notes and after completing the formalities of our interview she led me out to the barn to see various animals she was boarding.

Paula and I fell in love with a newly-born filly out of a mare called Bundle Baby. Teri also showed us a yearling colt by a son of Secretariat. She said if I was interested she could sell us the colt for $5,000. Further, if I would buy a mare in foal named Moonlight Drive for $10,000, she would throw in the filly suckling.

From the time a horse is born until it is weaned, it is called a "suckling." After it is weaned from its mother, the young horse becomes a "weanling" until January 1st of the next year when, regardless of its birthday, it becomes a yearling.

I was really anxious to start into the business and the thought of owning a relative of the great Secretariat was overwhelming. Little did I know that Secretariat had 646 foals, each of which could claim to be his son or daughter. If each of those foals then had 5 offspring, my colt could be one of 3,000 or more grandchildren.

That fact not withstanding, we agreed to purchase the colt for $5,000. Teri led us back into the house and signed over a bill of sale and told us that she would take care of the paperwork with The Jockey Club. At this point in time I had no idea what paperwork was required.

Because I am an attorney, my first inclination upon leaving the farm was to call The Jockey Club and find out what was involved in transferring title to a horse. I called the Lexington Kentucky office and spoke to a young woman who informed me of the following.

Each Thoroughbred, even before it is born, is registered in a report of breeding by the stallion's owner. After birth, the mare's owner is required to report to the state on the live birth of the foal.

Upon weaning the foal, The Jockey Club sends a blood kit which requires blood samples of the mother and foal, a description of the foal, a few photos and an application form to be filled out. Upon receipt of the same and the payment of a small fee, a certificate is issued.

In order to name the foal, six names must be submitted with the application, in descending order of preference.

If you want a monumental task, try to name a horse.

Almost every conceivable combination of names is already in use. With 47,000 births a year, finding a name is impossible.

This colt had been previously named. On the way home that day Paula and I decided to rename him, Motion Call. We would submit an application to The Jockey Club to change the name of the horse. This was permissible if the horse had not yet raced.

By the end of the day I was in business. I owned a horse and I had started my stable.

During the next week or so we visited the farm at least five times. Each time we came, Teri showed us the filly suckling and the mare in foal.

Teri told us she had a terminal illness and Paula and I were very taken by the fact that she was so young and her children would soon be without a mother. It appeared, from her conversation, that she would also lose the farm soon.

It seemed that if we purchased the mare and the suckling, regardless of their value, the money would be going to a good cause.

We decided to ask our good friends, Julie and Vito DePinto, if they wanted to share in this purchase.

Julie and Vito accompanied us out to the farm and we photographed Motion Call and played with the suckling and fed carrots to the mare. I think the DePintos were just as hooked as we were because, at the end of the day we, as a partnership, bought the mare in foal for $10,000. Teri, to her word, threw in the filly suckling.

My stable has now grown to three. Teri said she would only charge us $5 a day per horse for boarding for the first year. This sounded pretty reasonable.

The only negative aspect to this whole week was our

feelings toward Teri. There was something missing here. She was a rather confusing individual.

One day I came out to video the yearling, Motion Call, and she brought out the wrong horse. She claimed that she was on a very strong medication and couldn't see straight. Every time she tells me a fact or makes a promise of some sort it turns out to be different or never happens and there is always an excuse.

At this point I can honestly say I am very guarded. Somehow I don't think this will be the last time I will mention Teri in this book.

*"He is so big, to find him,*
*you look for a tree with hair."*

CHAPTER **4**

# MY PARTNER ROGER

The fall days of October began to replace the summer. The Arlington meet was coming to a close. I now had three horses. I was out $10,000 and I still was no closer to my goal. What I needed was both a partner and a horse that could earn money now.

Ernie called and said he had the perfect partner for me. His name was Roger Samson and that he was about 15 years my junior. Ernie said I'd like him because he was also Jewish. Ernie was interested in putting us together quickly because there were a couple of horses in a claiming race tomorrow that he wanted. Ernie told me to go to the horseman's bookkeeper at Arlington Park and deposit $10,000 and meet him at the track Saturday at about 12:30 p.m. I would meet my new partner. I asked Ernie for Roger's number so that I could talk to him first.

I called Roger that evening and we talked for about half an hour. My first impression of him over the phone was that we would get along quite well. I intended to go to the track with my good friend and client, Harold Saper on Saturday. I told Roger that we would meet him at the paddock area near the place where they stamp your hand to identify you when you return to the clubhouse. I am 6'2" and 225 pounds; and Harold goes a good 280 pounds and is 6'3". I told Roger to look for a couple of pretty big guys. Roger laughed and said, "Look for a tree with hair." It turned out that Roger is 6'4" and the only scale that can register his weight is usually found next to the tollway.

I met both Roger and Ernie at the paddock area as planned. Roger had deposited a matching $10,000 and Ernie said the play was to claim a certain 2-year old filly named Stone Harbor Jane. Roger and I were so proud that we were in the game that we both told betting clerks at Arlington about our intended claim.

This was to be our first team mistake. Roger is a pretty sophisticated horseman, having been involved for the past five years in the ownership of harness horses. I guess there is a difference between the two types of racing. Roger never had a fear of disclosing his intentions in harness racing to make a claim. However, I think our claiming intentions got back to the owners of Stone Harbor Jane because the horse was declared ill and withdrew from the race.

Ernie, Roger and I met and decided to claim a 2-year old filly in the same race named Our Tsunami Su. She would be running in the forth race with a claiming price of $20,000.

Watching that race was an exercise in composure. We wanted to believe that we would be claiming the best horse in the race. At the same time we didn't want her to win and break her maiden because we would not share in the prize money.

We watched the race from the rail near the finish line. I cannot express the feeling that I had during this race.

Each progressive step along the path to my goal carries with it a different feeling. This was similar to my first date.

The bell went off for the six furlong event and Our Tsunami Su broke sharply from the gate nose to nose with the leader. At the second call she was still second, only half a length off the leader with the jockey, Mark Guidry, holding her back for a big finish.

I might add at this point that, prior to this race, Our Tsunami Su, also a grandchild of Secretariat, had come in second twice to the best competition in the area and had been ridden by Hall of Fame jockey, Pat Day.

Turning for home she was still second, but in the final stretch, she tired and preserving fourth was the best she could do. Actually both Roger and I were thrilled. She had run a good race, come out of it sound and still had her maiden. After the race we visited our purchase for the first time. She was a nervous filly and after having run in a race would have nothing to do with us.

Paula and I went out that evening and we met Roger's wife, Dawn, for the first time. Dawn is an attractive young lady who bends the six foot mark. She and Roger have four children. Dawn was really into harness racing and was rather lukewarm to the idea of owning Thoroughbreds. Still, we seemed to hit it off right away and the four of us felt we were headed for a long friendship.

*"I never really liked this horse, and I always will."*

CHAPTER **5**

# OUR TSUNAMI SU

October 17, 1991, will be the first day that any horse I own will race under my own colors.

Prior to this time Dee, Roger and I met to design our silks. I can't say we had much of a design session. She asked what color we liked and I suggested a bright gold. Roger approved and we told Dee that a circle of black with our initials in it would be fine. So it would be F and S stables or S and F stables. We flipped a coin and from then on we would be The Forman and Samson Stables with a black F-S in a circle on the back of the silk.

Again Mark Guidry mounted Our Tsunami Su. We watched as she left the Hawthorne Race Course paddock with her mane braided and her bright blue bandages contrasting our gold colors. She was beautiful...the day was beautiful. This was the big show...and we were in it.

We drew the number 2 post position of 11 horses. This is what it is all about. The purse was $14,700 with $8,820 going to the winner. Roger and I spread about $600 on number 2 in perfecta keys. We went off as a 3/2 co-favorite. Stone Harbor Jane was also in the race.

Roger and I went down to the rail. The summer season at Arlington had ended and the two Cicero tracks, one of which is Hawthorne, would be our forum for the winter. The bell sounded and out they came, 11 maidens, only one of which would be victorious.

Tsunami broke alertly but was no match for Bobsho and at the first call was fifth. At the second call, she was third, only a half length off the high-flying leaders. Going into the first of two turns, our beautiful gold colors seemed to be going backwards as Bobsho, Life's Not Easy and Stone Harbor Jane battled for the lead. We watched as the horses finished one by one. Our heads kept turning to pick up the next finisher until we caught sight of our braided beauty completing the contest 25 1/2 lengths behind the winner.

We were ninth. Welcome to racing. Gone was the hope of gaining our first picture. Gone was the $600 we had bet. Zip, nada, was the return on our $20,000 investment.

Stone Harbor Jane had finished third and took home $1,600 for her efforts. Had we made a mistake? As Roger, Dawn, Paula and I left the track that day there was no joy in Mudville...Our Tsunami Su had struck out.

I don't know how Roger felt, but at least, I thought, we had tried. The horse returned healthy and there was always another day.

I began to remember how many people had told me I would go broke before I would win a stakes race or even get that first picture. I was beginning to doubt myself.

Charlie Bettis, Ernie's assistant trainer, called me. He thought he knew what was wrong with the horse. He had a vet put an instrument called a "scope" down her throat and found that there was a growth in her air passage that was preventing her from breathing properly. The veterinarian removed the obstruction and Charlie was going to train her in a different way and build her up. This meant no racing for about two months and only more bills from Ernie and the veterinarian, Dick Hume.

We had only run one race and already we had a horse in sick bay. Should I bail out now and give up or stick it out? I once heard the story of a farmer who won the lottery. They asked him what he would do with the millions of dollars he had just won. He said, "I think I'll keep farming until it runs out." I am beginning to feel like that farmer.

Dawn keeps telling Roger that he should have stuck to harness horses and gives him the "I told you so" bit. Paula has never questioned anything I have ever done and her confidence in me bolsters my own staying power. I am determined to stick this one out.

A little over a month passed. Ernie called me at 8:00 a.m. He told me that Our Tsunami Su was ready to run again and that she had worked great. I asked Ernie if she could win and he said, "Gonna be there."

Ernie would try to enter her in a maiden race for $13,200 on Thursday, December 5, in the fourth. We would know tomorrow about 1 p.m. if she had made the race. I know I am not going to sleep tonight.

On Tuesday we received the good news that we were in. The morning papers had her as the third favorite of 11 horses. We pulled the seven post. Enough reason to plunk down another $500.

My lucky numbers are seven, eight and thirteen. Pulling the seven post seemed an omen. Again, Tsunami paraded to the track with her braids and her blue stockings looking like a true princess. I saw a different horse today. She walked differently. She had more confidence and she now had a larger wind pipe.

Again, Mark Guidry mounted her. Ernie told him in the paddock, "save a little ground," meaning for him to take the horse to the rail and then pull back and make a late charge at the end of the race. This is the way Guidry likes to ride...from off the pace.

I desperately wanted to add in my own two cents worth, like an assistant coach in a huddle, but I didn't know enough about racing at this point to do anything but say, "Mark...give her a good ride...bring me home a picture."

The cement patio by the finish line was covered with ice and snow and Roger and I were the only people outside at the rail when the gates opened. Our wives had more sense and watched from inside with the other 3,000 spectators.

Out she came, second behind Ranvulera. The first quarter in :22 4/5 and only a half of a length off the lead. I thought her time was very fast for a horse trying to save ground. At the half mile marker in :47 2/5, a length behind the leading Ranvulera, who seemed to be pulling away now. On came Bileyas, an 18-1 shot, and challenged Tsunami for second as they headed home with Ranvulera now six to the good.

And then it happened. It now seems like it was all in slow motion. Guidry coaxed Tsunami to change leads. Down the middle of the track she flew. Past Bileyas, five lengths from the leader, then three. The finish line loomed up quickly as Tsunami caught the tiring Ranvulera and at the wire, there she was...Our Tsunami Su, all alone, two and a half-length victor in 1:13 3/5.

I didn't realize it then, but as the horses were heading toward the finish line all of them going west, I was running east to catch them. I had watched the finish of the race and then turned and headed west toward Roger standing there with his arms open. I leaped onto his gigantic frame and the two of us fell and rolled around in the snow in front of the racing audience who must have thought us a little loony.

And a little crazy I was. I do not remember taking that photo. But there it was now, on my desk. We had won almost $8,300 in the purse and another $2,000 in betting. There I was in the photo, in the winner's circle with a horse I owned. Only a short four months after my dream began.

Our Tsunami Su came out of that race a little sore. Ernie kept explaining to us that young fillies always get sore. She worked 1:07 2/5 for five eighths of a mile a week after the race, which to me, was pig slow for a workout. Ernie said, "They don't pay for workouts, forget it." His comments didn't encourage me, as I always look at a horse's workouts when placing a bet.

With the 1991 season drawing to a close, Ernie decided to take one last shot at a $13,000 race for non-winners of one race other than maiden or claiming. Here we were now facing horses all of which have won a race. The same names kept popping up, like George Getz's filly, Life's Not Easy. In the morning papers we were a second favorite behind Life's Not Easy at 4-1. By race time Tsunami was the favorite at 6-5. Life's Not Easy was 3-2. This was the featured eighth race. We had made the big time.

Bettors will tell you never to bet on a 2-year old filly after she has won her maiden race. The chances of back to back victories were slim to nil, however the bettors, including Roger and I, didn't see it that way. Boy, did we pound that betting window.

Every Christmas our family seems to end up at the Doral Country Club in Florida. The hotel chain was owned by Howard Kaskell, part owner of Life's Not Easy. This race was set up as a match race between these two young fillies. Two business moguls sending their steeds out to do battle. Big boys with big toys. I loved the concept.

Now, having won a race, I was prepared to lend my two cents into the pre-race conference. I told Guidry not to hold back and to try to use some of the speed of the young horse to our advantage. I am certain he listened to me with the same intensity as a 12-year old truant listens to his guidance counselor. Guidry is Guidry and would ride like Guidry. Anyway, it felt good to say something.

Again our colors sprang forth from the starting gate and again Guidry held the youngster back and settled her into fifth position on the rail. Mark looked over his shoulder at the first call and saw Juvenal Diaz, on Life's Not Easy, settling into ninth place. I could see their minds both working on their timing, waiting for the right moment to spring free and surprise the field.

Guidry made his move first. Moving into the turn, Our Tsunami kept her position in fifth place but was only half a length off the lead on the outside. This was absolutely perfect.

Again Guidry looked over his shoulder to see that he had not lost Diaz who was coaxing the Getz-trained filly to stay on our tail. Around the turn they came, the two favorites swinging to the outside preparing to overtake the field and break into their own two-horse race.

Unfortunately, no one conveyed these plans to

Running Sea and Sweet Luck. These two fillies withstood the challenge of the charging favorites while a late running Bethany's Brilliance took third. When the race ended, Tsunami had run fourth and Life's Not Easy a sorry fifth. A $768 check for fourth place money, and the minor success of having won our match race with Kaskell's filly, was all we left the track with that day. It took me a half-an-hour to clean my pockets of all of the losing tickets.

There is a sad but true comment to make relative to this race. Even though winter had set in, Roger and I persisted in watching the race outside. This was because of Roger's superstitions. Standing next to us, outside against the rail, was a tall thin man who had obviously bet on both Our Tsunami Su and Life's Not Easy in a perfecta box.

My guess is that it was his best bet of the day. This was one of the last races at Hawthorne and racing would not return for about a month-and-a-half when the season opened at Sportsman's Park. The racetracks were next door to each other in Cicero, Illinois and the only major difference between the tracks were that the purses offered at Sportsman's were considerably larger than at Hawthorne.

As it became apparent that neither Our Tsunami Su nor Life's Not Easy would win, the tall man ripped up his tickets and threw them in my direction. I am certain he didn't know that I was the owner of Tsunami, but since we were the only ones within ear shot to whom he could complain, he shouted, "It's just like some dem dam owners, to hold back the favorites so as to run dem next door for da big money."

No punishment was necessary as his monetary loss and the ignorance he would have to live with was sufficient retribution. However, this incident points out how the masses feel about the racing game. Every time someone loses, they think that the fix must be on. For the first time I was on the inside looking out and knew that there was no fix on. I wanted to win that race as much as any race I have or would ever run in, and I am certain that other owners always felt the same way in every race they ran in.

The racing season ended for me with that race. Our Tsunami Su was now as sore as ever and Charlie Bettis had become history with Ernie. It seems that Charlie had wanted a partnership or a better share of the profits since claiming that it was he and not Ernie who should be credited with the success of Black Tie Affair.

The relationship ended in a battle of words. Charlie went off to train on his own and Ernie hired an old trainer named Troy Patrick. Troy had some years on him and he didn't say much, but Ernie said he was one of the best leg men in the business. The change didn't affect me in any way, so only time will tell if this was a good move or not.

Our Tsunami Su stayed in the barn at Sportsman's Park during the winter receiving electrical stimulation, massage therapy, and all forms of wraps and salves, shots and medicines. All this and more at only $40 per day and again no income.

*"Admitting that you made a mistake is the hardest part of making one."*

CHAPTER **6**

# AND HERE
# COMES TERI

It didn't take long. As sure as I was sitting here I knew that Teri would enter my life again. As certain as I was about that fact, I was just as sure that it would mean trouble. But how much and how often I didn't know.

It was a few days before Christmas and Paula and I were about to leave for Florida with Steve and Diane Labkon. I couldn't wait to get to the sun and golf, and especially to the Doral Pro Am Golf tournament which I knew was always attended by Howard Kaskell. He may own everything in southern Florida, but I own a horse that beat his. That's as effective as saying, "My dad can beat up your dad." But it feels good.

Then a flood of phone calls started. The first call was from Julie De Pinto. She had gotten a phone call from a Mrs. Bunny Gora who claimed that the weanling filly belonged to her as well as the colt, Motion Call.

I called Mrs. Gora, who sounded like a very lovely woman who was very angry. She told me that she had boarded her mare, Bundle Baby with Teri. She said Teri had arranged the paperwork with The Jockey Club to make it look like Teri's farm, Duck Run, was the breeder of the two young horses when in fact, Bunny was.

Mrs. Gora wanted her horses back. After a lengthy conversation with her, I told her I would speak to Teri about the situation and get back to her.

I was just about to contact Teri when call number two came in. A man, identifying himself as Dr. Chris, told me the mare that was in foal had been bred to Bruce Duchossois's Media Star Guest and that there was a $2,500 stud fee still owing to Hill 'N Dale Farm.

I pulled my purchase records and found a bill of sale from Teri which stated on its face that the stud fees had been prepaid. It had been signed by Teri. I wrote down Dr. Chris's phone number and told him I would call him back.

I called Teri to make an appointment to meet her so that we could straighten out the difficulties. I thought I was about to lose my filly and my colt and owe even more money on an already overvalued mare. Teri was too sick to talk to me. She kept mumbling about losing the farm and told me that I would have to move my animals, which I was not sure were still mine. This meant bringing the horses to a real farm which could run us upwards of $16 per horse per day. When I couldn't get Teri to meet with me I told her I would call back and I hung up.

I then called my partner in the mare and filly, Julie. I told her that Teri was about to lose the farm and that we would have to move the horses which meant more expenses. Since Teri had promised Julie a $5 a day rate, Julie was not happy with the idea of added expenses and wanted out.

I bought out Julie's share in the horses for the same price she had paid. I didn't want to take any chances with

Teri losing the farm and the horses disappearing. Within a few hours of the phone calls I called Ernie who arranged to have the three horses sent to Horizon Farm in Barrington, Illinois.

The next day when the horses arrived they were inspected for diseases and put into quarantine. Dave Noby of Horizon called to tell me that the horses were healthy and that the mare no longer was carrying twins. One had died. This was the first time I had heard anything about twins.

This news hit me like a lightning bolt. Rarely can a horse carry twins. When twins are discovered, either you destroy one of the fetus's by pinching it off, or the mare and both foals stand a good chance of not surviving. I had been sold a $10,000 corpse. When I bought the mare I had no idea I was to order an examination from a veterinarian. I never thought that an ex-groom of Ernie's would ever cheat one of his clients.

In retrospect, this was good news. Even though I now owe more money on this mare, in the form of a stud fee, the probability of a live birth was ensured. On the other hand, I had been duped. I was the patsy, the fool, the mark. It just goes to show you that God does protect the infirm and the stupid and that even a blind squirrel finds a nut now and then.

I had been tricked into one of the best deals I had made so far. Dave said that the breeding on the weanling was damn good and she was straight and healthy and I had made a darn good deal.

That's great, but it still left me with the problem of Bunny Gora and her claim to the two young horses. I called Bunny again who disclosed that she could not afford a commercial barn and with Teri going out of business, she would not be able to afford to keep the two young horses.

I entered into a written agreement with Bunny. The title to the horses would be changed to reflect her as the breeder. In the event the horses won any money, she would get the Breeders' awards. Further, I would move the weanling to a farm nearer to her called Regal Creek in Harvard, Illinois, where she could also move her mare, Bundle Baby. She could visit the young horse and watch it grow. In the event the horse ran for a claiming price she could purchase the horse for that price from me directly.

I still had to meet with Teri and find out what she had to say about all of this. I made an appointment to visit her on Sunday. Then the next call came. It was Liberty Tack Shop. I had ordered a blanket and halter for Motion Call. I made the mistake of letting Teri call and I gave her my credit card number. All sorts of tack had been ordered on my card which did not belong to me.

I convinced Liberty Tack that I didn't owe them the sum of money they said I did and I reversed the charges with my credit card company.

Even though we were leaving that night for Florida, I felt compelled to visit Teri. This would be my last visit with her.

I again entered the house with the death smell. As usual Teri was sprawled out on the couch with a blanket over her, sucking on ice cubes. She laid a trip on me about her cancer and her terminal condition and regardless of how I approached the subject or what the subject was, she had an answer or had a document hidden in some cabinet that she could not get into right now which would offer me the proof that I needed.

I told her that even though we had never established an attorney/client relationship and that she had never paid me a retainer, I did not wish her to feel that at any time I was her lawyer. I made it clear that I would not perform any work on any of her complaints and that she should seek other counsel.

I asked her about Bunny Gora and she responded that Bunny had never paid her board and that the colt and filly were left as collateral.

I asked her about the mare and about her knowing that the mare was carrying twins. She denied any knowledge of this. She was adamant in insisting that Dr. Chris had received a free stud service from Hill N' Dale and that I owed no money.

I politely took my leave, wished her a good life and parted from Teri forever. I now knew why Dee cringed at the very sound of her name.

I returned home and called Dr. Chris. I found out that Hill N' Dale had taken the stud fee off his bill as their veterinarian. When I agreed to split the stud fee with him he jumped at the offer. I sent him a check and left for Florida.

You may think that only so much shit can cover only so much fan at one time. When I arrived in Florida there was a call from Ernie. He had been served a summons to appear in court to answer charges of having co-signed a note for $15,000 for Teri from a bank in Aurora, Illinois.

I promised Ernie I would represent him. Ernie said he wanted to talk to me about a new horse. I begged off. I had heard all I wanted to about horses and Teri and farms and bills. I wanted to golf.

*"When you get a chance to throw your first pitch
in the big leagues, throw it down the middle."*

CHAPTER **7**

# TEN TAYLOR ROAD

I guess that when I get involved in an activity, I really get involved. Not even Florida was a safe haven from horse racing. I didn't even have the chance to lose my first golf ball before I was again confronted with a decision.

Evidently Ernie must have had a pretty good idea that Our Tsunami Su would shortly be history, because he began calling me long distance about buying a new horse or claiming one. Somehow he never called Roger. Ernie knew that if I approved the horse Roger would fall in line. Then Ernie stopped calling, and strangers from all across the United States started calling with deals.

We were still in Florida and it was just before New Year's Eve when I received a call from a man whose name I cannot remember. He invited me out to Gulfstream Park to see a horse that he said would be able to blow away everything in Chicago. Not having much experience in the field I went.

Gulfstream Park was closed, but the barns were being used to board racehorses. I met the gentleman and viewed the horse in question. I only mention this here because of the stupid feeling I had when I confronted this animal face to face. What was I to do? He had no tires to kick. Should I look at his teeth? Do I ask him to run?

I looked around the stall a few times and hemmed and hawed, I shook my head up and down, and side to side. Nothing was in my head at the time, but I didn't want the horse broker to think I didn't know anything. I asked the broker to supply me with the horse's pedigree and race records and asked if I could hire a veterinarian to examine him.

Even though this was done almost immediately, I turned down the deal. Not because the horse was sick or lame or not a good deal, but because I had no idea what I was doing and not a clue as to what I was looking for.

By mid-January, we were back in Northbrook. Our Tsunami Su was still sore, but Ernie said we would try to run her at Sportsman's Park in February. I didn't have much hope for a comeback for her and my dreams of a stakes horse were fading. Motion Call would not be ready to run for at least a year. The filly, whom we named after my daughter, Missy's Shystar, was two years away from running and the mare wouldn't foal until April or May.

Ernie persisted in calling with deals. $150,000, $100,000, what did he think I was made of? Would it take a monumental amount of money to buy a winner? His persistence at least afforded me an opportunity to look over a ton of pedigrees and race records and I began to get a feeling of what I was looking for. I had turned down so many horses that I began to feel that Ernie would give up on me.

It was midday, January 25, I was at work and had left my gloves on my desk and came back for them. That, perhaps, is the only reason I was in my office to receive Dee's call that morning. I was in quite a rush to get to court but I would never fail to answer a call from Dee.

She said that a fellow named Steve Specht had spotted several horses with potential in California that were running in claiming races at Bay Meadows. Dee said that she could fax me what information she had on the horses if I was interested. If I wanted any of the horses I would need to debit wire transfer the cash immediately, to make the claim, as the races were the next day.

I filtered through the faxed material and pulled two horses from the group, one filly and one gelding. The filly was Nasty Temptation, a 4-year old and the gelding was a 3-year old named Ten Taylor Road.

I was immediately impressed with the gelding's pedigree. His sire was Kennedy Road, twice named Horse of the Year in Canada. The sire had earned over $480,000 and had sired 21 black-type winners. (When a horse wins a stakes race that fact is recorded in bold black type so as to stand out in a pedigree). I knew that 15 of the last 25 derby winners were from the Nearco line and 11 of them through Nasrullah. This horse qualified.

Upon examining his race record I found that he had only run three times as a 2-year old. His very first race was against open competition including some of the best in the west. He came in 10th, only nine lengths from the leader. His next two races were maiden races in which he had come in second no more than two lengths from the leader. The times of all of his races were impressive. The horse was jet black, not too big and not too small. The claiming price was $20,000, just right.

This was to be my choice. I canceled my next few

appointments and made haste to the bank to wire-transfer the money to a bank in Arcadia, California. I called Roger and his response to me was, "did you check it over?...is it good?" Since my response to both questions was affirmative, Roger had no problem making the deal. Roger is the easiest guy in the world to be a partner with.

My next call was to a gentleman friend who knew someone who could take a wager on the race long distance.

Ten Taylor Road ran third in that race on January 25. Roger and I had been successful in claiming him. It would cost us an additional $2,700 each over the purchase price for Specht's commission and for air freight home.

Ten Taylor Road flew into Chicago that next Monday and was immediately taken to Sportsman's Park in Cicero. Paula, Dawn, Roger and I visited our purchase.

Upon entering the barn at Sportsman's we stopped first at Our Tsunami Su's stall. All the other horses in the barn—all 40 or 50 of them—were facing head out looking at us as we passed by with curiosity. There was Tsunami, tail out. We called out her name and she wouldn't even acknowledge our presence. I really hoped that our new gelding would be a lot friendlier.

We left Tsunami and one stall at a time we visited the five new purchases. These five California imports were supposed to tear up the track at Sportsman's this spring and we owned one of them.

We came to Ten Taylor Road's stall. There was this little black horse who was all legs. His hind feet had white stockings and there was a faint white mark on his forehead, the only contrasting marks on an otherwise jet black coat. He was a little drugged from the flight and could only manage to stare sleepily at his new owners.

Right now it doesn't seem possible that this tired little puppy will fulfill my dream. But only time will tell.

A week has passed and Ernie still has not breezed our new horse. He says the horse is not eating well yet and is still getting acquainted with the new track. They are galloping him every day. I asked about Our Tsunami and Ernie said we would try to find her a race this week. He told me to have patience on our new purchase and when the time was ready I wouldn't be disappointed.

We found a race for Our Tsunami Su that week. This was a $14,000 race for non-winners of two races. We were the morning line co-favorite at 2-1. It was a sloppy, cloudy day. We drew the 10 hole, which should help us on a muddy track. Strangely enough, just as our race was going off, the clouds separated and the sun came out. Would this be a good omen?

Again Mark Guidry took our colors to the post. Again Tsunami ran the kind of race we were getting used to. She settled into the middle of the pack, made a late charge and came up two lengths short of victory, in third. We cashed $1,600 for this effort and at least had this month's feed money.

Immediately after the race, Ernie was thumbing through the new racing schedule and said, "Good news, I got a race for the gelding." Ten Taylor Road was to run this Friday. February 21, we were entered in the seventh, a maiden race for 3 and 4-year olds. Ernie said we would "blow this field away." The morning line had us as the second favorite at 3-1.

The day was bright and rather warm for mid-

February. The winner's purse of $9,000 would go nicely with the $1,600 that Tsunami had made. Hopefully, with both horses running, it might be possible to pull in an average of over $1,000 a week for a couple of months.

When Ten Taylor appeared in the paddock for the first time I could not believe my eyes. The little black horse had turned, over night, into the most beautiful and athletic gelding I had ever laid my eyes on. A white number 4 stood out boldly against his jet black body and the contrast of our black and gold colors made a perfect match.

Again our jockey, Mark Guidry, mounted the gelding and off to battle they went. As we walked to the grandstand to watch the race, I saw Earl Silver, an old high school chum. Wouldn't you know it, he had a horse in the same race, by the name of Silken Road. Ten Taylor Road against Silken Road, this was too much.

Roger and I pounded the betting windows. It would be feast or famine. $500 across and a $20 perfecta wheel up and down.

Off they went. Guidry did everything humanly possible to settle the horse into second or third to make a-Guidry-run-for-home. The young gelding would have nothing to do with this plan. No matter how hard Guidry tried to stay off the lead, the strong willed Ten Taylor Road went to the front and stayed there.

Guidry kept looking over his shoulder trying not to lose the field. As the field rounded the final turn and headed for home, I waited for Mark to make his final move with the horse. Instead he seemed content to allow the field to catch him in so they would spend themselves. From this position, Guidry felt he could call on the gelding at the final pole and pull away from the field.

A horse, bearing the number 3, made a run at Ten Taylor from the outside. Ten Taylor caught sight of the fast approaching rival and lugged to the right, 15 feet or so, and put what looked like a hockey check on the other horse.

"Oh shit," was all that Roger could say as he dropped his binoculars from his eyes. "They're gonna take us down." (Which means if we finish first they will disqualify our horse for bumping the other horse).

Right after the bump, the number 3 horse went sideways and slowed. Ten Taylor Road went on to an easy six and a half length victory. The three horse was Earl Silver's Silken Road.

We had won our first race with Ten Taylor Road. Well, we won for at least 10 minutes. Immediately after Mark returned from the phone call from the stewards, the numbers 4 and 3 were reversed on the score board. We had been taken down. We were second for a purse of $3,000 instead of $9,000. I walked over to Earl, who was glad to have won, but who was, on the other hand, gentleman enough to recognize my pain. We congratulated each other and I kiddingly told him, "you owe me six grand." We never even took a picture. It was now the beginning of March. We were on a roll now. We only hoped that Tsunami would return to form. What an incredible feeling it would be to have two horses running at the same time and winning. It was not to be. Tsunami ran forth in a field of eight and cashed $1,300 for her effort. Gone was the final kick and gone was the spark in her eyes. This was a filly who wanted out.

Ten Taylor came out of the last race in pretty good condition, but Ernie mentioned something about his right front ankle being a little hot after the race.

Every time we tried to enter him into a race, the race didn't fill. We finally made it into a race, but just prior to the race the rest of the card was canceled by the jockeys. They complained that the management had put down some type of agent on the track to keep it from freezing, and the material was burning the horses and kicking up into the faces of the jockeys. March 18th was a sunny Wednesday. Ten Taylor Road was entered into the second race, a $14,700 purse race for maidens. We pulled the 10 post. Ernie told us that Guidry was already riding the favorite in the race, Love Them Kisses. We hired a youngster by the name of E.T. Baird to ride. E.T.'s father, Bobby Baird, was at one time one of the best jockeys in the business. Bobby was now E.T.'s agent.

Ernie told E.T. that there was too much speed in the race, and that he would have to save a little. I told E.T. to take the horse out to the lead. Ernie told me to mind my own business, in a polite way.

Ten Taylor Road broke alertly. He settled into second and then third. The favorite, Love Them Kisses, and the speed in the race, Silver Royalty, set up a match race. Ten Taylor pressed the leaders until the eighth pole and then exploded past the favorite at the wire. We won our first race with Double T's (my nickname for Ten Taylor Road). Paula and Dawn had missed the race. Strangely enough, Ernie's wife Dee was also absent. I had driven to the race with my son, Spencer. When we lined up for the photo, only men stepped forth. It was kind of a nice bonding to share with your partner and son. Another $8,800 rung up in the till along with a rather healthy win at the windows. This was becoming fun. We were no longer scratching for feed money. We were earning some serious coin of the realm. I started to calculate what this type of return could do for us on an annual basis.

It was now the middle of March. Our Tsunami Su was entered in a $14,700 race for non-winners of two. She was 5-1 at post time as the third favorite in a field of nine.

Out she came and went right for the lead. There they were, five horses across the track head to head for the first three furlongs. Then, pop. Our bubble burst. For the first time since our maiden race we failed to cash. Tsunami fell back to sixth. No purse, no prize money, no photo, no hopes of a stakes winner. Something is wrong. This is not how I had planned it.

Back in the paddock Ernie gave us the bad news. The filly's knee was gone or at least the cartilage between the bones, which meant that the horse was incapable of competing any longer. Ernie planned to dump her in a claiming race hoping that someone would take her off of our hands. Tsunami Su had become a liability.

All our hopes and dreams would be on Ten Taylor Road's back. How far could we go with a one-horse barn?

CHAPTER **8**

# A PART OF A
# DREAM COME TRUE

April Fools! This can't be true. I just hung up from speaking to Ernie. He has Ten Taylor Road entered in a stakes race. An honest to goodness $50,000 added stakes race for 3-year olds. Since Ten Taylor's sire was Kennedy Road, a Breeders' Cup eligible stallion, our gelding was eligible for this race.

The Breeders' Cup is best known as the championship of Thoroughbred racing. But the championship day is just one facet of a multi-million dollar stakes racing program which benefits the Thoroughbred industry on a year-round basis. The program includes two other important components: the Breeders' Cup Budweiser Special Stakes Program and the Breeders' Cup Premium Stakes Program.

Started in 1986, the Breeders' Cup Budweiser Special Stakes Program is a series of 50 stakes races held at more than 40 racetracks. The Premium Stakes Program, instituted in 1989, provides purse money for stakes races at nearly every racetrack in the U.S. and Canada. Approximately 150 races a year are supplemented in this way.

My dream was to win a graded stakes race. Now,

granted, this was not THE Breeders' Cup Classic, but it was the "Lost Code Breeders' Cup Stakes" with $30,000 going to the winner as well as a Breeders' Cup trophy, which to me would be like winning an Oscar.

What was equally as thrilling is that we started to get press. Our names were printed in the sports section of the newspaper as well as in the nationally published racing news. Well, we didn't get headlines. All the headlines went to the favorite, Gee Can He Dance. Three columns devoted to Betty Gabriel's horse. At the end of the article it said, "Completing the Lost Code cast...Dawn and Roger Samson and Lee Forman's Ten Taylor Road."

Some day soon, those turkeys will be asking for an interview. As for now we'll settle for "completing the field."

Saturday, April 4 was the most memorable day in my racing career to date. What an incredible thrill to stand in the paddock area as the owner of a horse entered in a stakes race. The television camera panned by us and I knew that the guys at the OTB's could see me on TV.

E.T. was again selected by Ernie to ride Double T's. After all, he had won on the horse and Guidry was riding another horse in the race. Bobby Baird couldn't be happier. He was looking for his son to link up with a reputable owner with a great mount who could put his son on the board. Maybe we were the ones.

An interesting sidelight to Bobby Baird. As an agent he is not allowed in the photograph of the win. There is a rule against it among agents. Sort of like illegal advertising. Bobby manages to get himself positioned behind the photo so that he is not in the front of the photo but always in the background. This is reminiscent of Alfred Hitchcock. When

I found out about it, I examined my one win photo of Ten Taylor Road and sure enough, there was Bobby.

E.T. was bright-eyed and bushy-tailed and willing to listen to anybody and anything. Ernie was strangely silent. I actually gave the rider instructions. Ernie looked at me, laughed and said, "Don't worry, he'll be there."

The only thing that ran through my mind was that my partner Roger was out of town and would not know about the results until I called him.

Neither the racing fans nor sports writers seemed to agree with Ernie. The morning press had us at best a 20-1 long shot. The betters brought us down to 13-1.

I was fearless at the windows. I bet $500 to win and $500 to place. I keyed Ten Taylor in the pick 9 and took a rather large perfecta box with the favorite Gee Can He Dance. The Gabriel horse had already earned $86,000 and we had just won our first race.

I made my bets and climbed into the stands. I positioned myself standing on a chair abeam the finish line.

Clang! the bell sounded, and the familiar voice of Phil Georgeff cried, "annnnnnnd they'rrrrr off!" I was partially blocked by a pillar but I heard the first call go to Ten Taylor Road. Our horse had exploded out of the number five stall and was leading the speed, De La Concorde and Gee Can He Dance, with fractions of :22 2/5 at the first call and :45 3/5 at the second call.

Our gold colors stood out against the blue winter sky in a flaming contrast resembling the setting sun. "And here they come spinning out of the turn," came the familiar Georgeff cry. Ten Taylor was in the lead now by two lengths. Only 100 yards to go and we were still winning. Only the

Gabriel mount, Gee Can He Dance, was left to challenge us. On he came. All that I can remember was his white hood, bobbing up and down. He looked like a Ku Klux Klan member chasing our black horse.

The finish line seemed to be moving away from us as in slow motion we watched the ground between the two horses being eaten up by the big chestnut. Just as Ten Taylor was about to be caught, just yards from the finish line, I swear he looked over his shoulder and saw the charging favorite. Ten Taylor Road dug deep down into his young heart, bowed his head to gather his strength and to the cadence of E.T.'s whip crashing into his flank came up with one last valiant lunge at the finish line. I can hear the voice of Georgeff echoing in my ears again and again…"It's all Ten Taylor Road…It's all Ten Taylor Road."

A horse I owned had won a stakes race. We were in the winner's circle just as I had dreamed, accepting the heavy bronze Breeders' Cup trophy and the prize money of over $33,000.

The camera flashed once, twice, again. I saw the TV camera pan by and I raised the trophy for all to see. It was over in an instant. No Roger to knock down, but Julie and Vito were there and the four of us hugged in the winner's circle. I wanted to hug Ten Taylor also but he was led away so fast by Troy that I didn't even get to slap him on the neck.

A racing official handed us the victory blanket and invited us to join the president of the racetrack in his private office for a drink. We were escorted quickly to a private elevator and led up to the sanctum of Charles W. Bidwill Jr., known to the racing industry as "Stormy."

Upon entering the inner chambers, we were greeted

by a thin, white-haired, bearded gent who was elegant and impressive. "Stormy" invited us to a glass of wine and replayed the race on his VCR. After the replay, he removed the tape and handed it to me as a token from the racetrack. About the same exact time that we were completing the formalities, a young horse by the name of A.P. Indy, ridden by Eddie Delahoussaye, was winning the simulcasted Santa Anita Derby from California.

I needed that win to complete the pick six that day which was good for an additional $675. I had boxed the ticket four ways and the teller paid me $2,700. Ten Taylor paid $29.20 to win and the perfecta paid an additional $119.40. I had hit a vein of pure gold. My pockets were loaded with hundred dollar bills and both hands were needed to carry the video tapes and the two trophies for Roger and me.

I learned a good lesson today. Up to this point, every time I go to the track I have taken money from some of my friends to bet on my horse. When someone knows you have a horse running they almost invariably say something like, "Say, will you bet five across on him for me?" Then they search through their wallets and find themselves a bit short and tell you that they will pay you back after the race. What now seems worse are those who actually give you the money.

Before coming to the track today we saw Harold and Glenda Saper. Glenda gave me $10 to bet on Ten Taylor Road to win. In all the excitement of the TV cameras and pre-race preparation I forgot to place her bet.

When we saw them that night, she gave me a big hug and a kiss and held out her hand for her 13-1 windfall. When I saw her hand out I remembered not placing the bet and I faked the excitement and took out a $120 of my own money and paid her.

From now on whenever anyone asks me to bet on my horse, even my best friend, my answer will be that I cannot.

What is worse, is that some of the cheapskates that told me to bet five across never paid me when they lost, but they were the first ones on the phone when they won.

Upon leaving the track that day I realized what had happened. I set out to do something and my goal was getting closer. Although this was not a graded stakes, it most certainly was a day in my life I shall never forget.

On the way home I dialed Roger's out-of-town number. No one answered. I had been instructed that if I couldn't reach Roger that I was to leave a message on his car phone answering service.

I dialed his number and after listening to Roger's recorded message, I spoke, "Roger, this is Lee. We just left the racetrack and I have some good news and some bad news for you...The bad news is that you missed the race...The good news is we won the fucking Lost Code Breeders' Cup...See you soon."

It took Roger less than an hour to call me back. "You're screwing with my mind," is all that he could say. "Naw...we didn't win did we?" I swore on my kid's life, which was the only way I could convince him that we had won. If it is possible to hug over the phone, we did it that day.

You should see the collection of newspaper clippings I have now. No longer were we "...also running is Ten Taylor Road." We were now, "HAS ERNIE GOT ANOTH-ER BIG ONE?" and "LIFE AFTER BLACK TIE IS STILL A BALL." I can't believe they are writing about Ten Taylor

Road, my horse.

Neil Milbert in the Tribune wrote, "Poulos was back in the Chicago limelight last weekend when Ten Taylor Road, a three-year-old gelding he claimed for $20,000 in California in February, scored an upset victory in the $51,950 Lost Code Breeders' Cup Stakes at Sportsman's Park." 'Hey, we may go all the way to the Illinois Derby!' exclaimed Poulos afterward," he wrote.

We have only owned the horse since January 25 and all he has done for us is cross the finish line three times in first place.

The Daily Racing Form chanted, "The 37th running of the $100,000 Thomas D. Nash Memorial Handicap, grade 3 will renew the rivalry that began in the Lost Code between Forman and Samson's Ten Taylor Road and Betty Gabriel's Gee Can He Dance."

The most exciting of the many articles written appeared in the Daily Racing Form. John Brokopp's Turf Tails carries a headline, "TEN TAYLOR ROAD NEXT POULOS STAR?" The article proclaimed, "Ten Taylor Road has a long, long way to go before he fills the shoes of Black Tie Affair but he took a step in the right direction last Saturday when he scored an upset victory in the Lost Code Breeders' Cup Stakes."

Everyday it was another headline, "POULOS HEADS WEST, RETURNS WITH GEM: TEN TAYLOR ROAD," "TEN TAYLOR ROAD, THE SECOND COMING OF BLACK TIE AFFAIR," "TEN TAYLOR ENTERED INTO FROST KING PURSE, SAME DAY AS NASH."

Whoa, that last headline floored me. Had Ernie gone soft in the head. He entered us into the Nash and into an allowance race at the same time on the same day.

I asked Ernie what he had in mind and he said that it was an old racing trick. If the field came up too heavy for us he would withdraw and run in the allowance race. However, the news media was too smart for Ernie. They caught on and published his tricks as soon as he pulled them.

We now were looking forward to April 18, and the running of a graded stakes race, the Nash Memorial. Would my dream be realized this soon? Would Ten Taylor win a graded stakes race and become a "big horse"? I would set aside this thought and concentrate on Our Tsunami Su who would run in her first claiming race, a paltry $16,000 affair on April 9. Would this be the end of Our Tsunami? was a more pertinent question.

*"The perfect horse should have three buttons
on its head that read: On; Win; and Off."*

CHAPTER **9**

# OUR TSUNAMI SU
# BIDS ADIEU

April 9 was a dreary Thursday. Compared to the excitement that was involved with Ten Taylor Road, it seemed like just another day at the racetrack. Ernie had Tsunami X-rayed and the verdict was a total loss of cartilage in one of her knees. Ernie shot her with some kind of snake venom to act as a cushion. We couldn't convince any of our top choices to ride her but Ernie persuaded Kerwin Clark to accept the ride. Kerwin had been a top gun at one time but now was humble enough to accept a ride such as this from Ernie.

I will not glorify this race with a call. When all was said and done, Our Tsunami Su had run seventh, 13 lengths behind the winner and again was sore after the race.

Ernie, Roger and I discussed how to handle the situation. It was decided that we would drop her to a $5,000 claimer as soon as she was physically able to make it to the paddock, ease her through the race and see if some schmuck would claim her. Now this seems a bit seedy I know, but this is how the game is played and I am just learning, and these are not my ideas.

There is a lot of greed out there and when someone notices an allowance horse dropping that far in class they know something is wrong. However, from time to time a gem is picked up that way. Ernie picked up The King's Sloop for $10,000. Dave Feldman laughed Ernie off the front page of the sports section in the Sun Times. After the King's 10th win, I think Dave stopped laughing. The King had won more than 10 times his purchase price and still no one would touch him in a claiming race. They all thought his next race would surely be his last.

When Charlie Bettis left Ernie, he took the King and sure enough the first race Charlie ran him in was the King's last.

Anyway, running Tsunami in a low class claimer was the only way to move her. I think I will complete the story of Our Tsunami out of chronological order because it doesn't have an exciting finish.

We had entered a May 6 race where Our Tsunami Su, proud granddaughter of Secretariat, would run against dog meat. She drew post 9 of 10 horses. Even Kerwin Clark wouldn't accept a ride. It was either an unknown by the name of Marquez or me. If I rode, which is pure fantasy, we would certainly hear the announcement, "Our Tsunami Su...now 108 pounds over."

They popped Marquez into the saddle and led him to the slaughter. I asked Ernie if I should bet on the race. He said, "Yeah, bet her to live...she'll go off at 10-1." With that he gave a gigantic belly laugh and said, "She's lucky to make it around the track."

To show you how uninformed the public is, they made her a 5-1 third choice. I went upstairs in the owners' club room to watch the race. There is no sense in getting cold watching a slaughter. I told someone that if she won I would jump down into the winner's circle by parachute.

As I approached the betting window a certain auto dealer, whose name shall not be disclosed, (as I know he would not sign off on a release of this story) approached me and asked why I was running her so cheap. I reminded him of Ernie and The King's Sloop and I said he would have to guess along with the other thousands of people whether she was dead meat or running out of class.

He offered me $4,000 on the spot for the horse and asked me to split whatever prize money she won in this race. I asked him in front of a dozen witnesses if he was serious and after he said yes we shook hands on the deal. He then said that he preferred to pay by check, which he didn't have on him at the time, and he would send me one and have his trainer take the horse right after the race.

I ran downstairs to tell Ernie and Roger. Ernie asked me what kind of line I fed him. I said that I had said absolutely nothing. He smiled, and patted me on the ass, like a major second story man congratulating his young pickpocket son on his first acquisition.

The purchaser's trainer came over and asked Ernie if there was anything wrong with the horse. Ernie mumbled something which sounded like an answer. He didn't lie but at the same time he didn't say, "Well to tell you the truth, the horse is missing cartilage in one knee and might not make it around the track." What he said sounded like, "Tssss O.K."

The gate opened and I think it must have hit Tsunami in the head. She stumbled out and went into a dying act that Sarah Bernhardt could have won an academy award for. When the race was over they had to send out a search party for her.

There at the finish line was the schmuck auto dealer. One by one he watched as the horses finished until he saw Tsunami literally walk across the finish line and limp back to the paddock led by a groom.

"I'll send you a check after my vet checks her out," were his last words to me. The check never came.

I now had a racehorse that was 3 years old and incapable of racing. I boarded her at Regal Creek in Harvard, Illinois with Peggy and Geoff Matson. Peggy nursed the mare back to a reasonable state of health and when I visited the horse in June, she let me pet her head, feed her carrots and I even hugged her good-bye.

Off the track she was one happy puppy. Her knee had healed enough so that she could be ridden and would be able to live a full healthy life away from the track.

I donated Tsunami to the Lakeshore Academy, which will use her for those disabled children who are unfortunate enough not to be able to afford a horse. She will be well cared for and groomed and loved. Fortunately, because of the care Ernie gave this horse and the jock's decision to pull her up in the race before she became permanently disabled, she came out of the race relatively uninjured but not capable of competing any longer in racing.

Our Tsunami Su provided me with my first racing win and I will never forget her for that. A large photo of that first win adorns my trophy wall in the center of all the other photos.

In passing, and as a final tribute to this brave filly, I will always remember her in that first win especially because of the way that Phil Georgeff slaughtered her name in that race. She started out as Our Tsunami Su. On the first turn she was Tsunami Slew. Spinning out of the turn she became Tsunami Stew and as Mark Guidry made that fabulous late charge, Phil shouted out…"and its all OUR SALAMI STEW."

*"You know you're in trouble when your nose runs
more than your horse."*

CHAPTER **10**

# A GRADED STAKE

It wasn't very long after the win in the Lost Code that I received a call from Ernie. "We're gonna try the Nash," he said over the phone. Somehow, the words didn't register. "What's the Nash?" was my reply. Ernie could have explained the race in 15 languages, the only fact that I heard was that it was a graded stakes race. Oh my God! A graded stake race. Could my goal be reached this soon.

The race would be run April 18 at Sportsman's Park. The newspaper articles began appearing again. Ten Taylor Road was regarded as one of the favorites in a graded stake race.

Let's return to earth for a moment. I took great pains to explain that a graded stakes race is the ultimate dream of any horse owner. There are different levels of graded races, the most highly regarded being a grade 1 race.

The Nash Memorial Handicap is a grade 3 race. This would make a race like the Nash only two steps from the top class of racing in America.

Any horse that could win a graded stake race at any level could easily be classified as being in the top 100 or so horses in America in that age group. Now, I suppose there are some who would dispute that fact but I know from the texts that I have read that there are almost 47,000 horses born each year with the intention of racing and that the average horse during its lifetime only earns $1,000. Up to this point, Ten Taylor Road had earned a few pennies over $50,000 and he was still just starting his sophomore year of racing. That fact alone would stand as prima facia proof in any argument that Roger and I owned a world class gelding.

The Nash was also a little different inasmuch as it would cost us $100 to subscribe to the race. An additional $250 would be paid to pass the entry box and $500 is due at scratch time which is 48 hours before race time. We would be at risk for $850.

Imagine the thrill I felt when I picked up the morning newspaper and read about, "Dawn and Roger Samson, and Lee and Paula Forman's Ten Taylor Road." I stare at the bold type now and remember back in August of 1991 sitting down at my computer and typing thoughts like, "How does one who is 51 years old get into the newspaper or record books?" and "I would learn all there was to know about horse racing, purchase a horse and win a stakes race."

Now, only a short eight months later, after having gained an education and purchased a few horses, I was reading my name in the sports section and a horse I owned was entered in a graded stakes race. Somehow in the back of my mind I knew that this had been too easy. Somewhere, somehow, some way my bubble was going to burst.

I am going to remain excited but also reserved. I am not going to expect the worst to happen, but I am sure going to be looking over my shoulder. Somewhere there is going to be a bump in the road and I am not going to be looking in the other direction when I hit it.

I spent the entire night on the computer trying to calculate our chances of winning the Nash. Let me tell you something about handicapping. You can convince yourself of anything in the world. There is enough information to justify almost any result. Five experts can meet and select five different winners in a single race and each of them can convince you that they are right. My computer selected our horse as one of the top three in the field of seven. The purse is $100,000. Jesus Christ, a $100,000 dollars. $60,000 plus to the owner of a horse which can run the fastest. To borrow an expression from Yakov Smirnoff, "What a country."

Even third place would pay somewhere between $11,000 and $13,000. That is comparable to first money in most of the allowance races we had been running in.

The morning papers have us at 2-1 with Gee Can He Dance the favorite at 4-5. Ten Taylor had just beaten the Gabriel stallion less than two weeks ago.

One horse in the race was getting a tremendous amount of press. Lou Goldfine's Danc'n Jake. The horse had only won $27,000 lifetime but had run second to Technology at Gulfstream and third to Saint Ballardo. Those two horses could, at this time, be rated at the top of the list of the best 3-year olds in the nation.

"Jake" had just been gelded because he couldn't keep his mind on racing and was doing a lot of stupid things on the track. If Goldfine's decision to geld was right, this horse could be tough to beat. Ten Taylor Road had just begun to shed his greenness himself and we had no idea if he could run with this class of horses.

I wore my best suit to the track with my lucky tie.

Paula bought me a Joe Sherman tie with all forms of horse racing memorabilia handpainted on it. The tie was loud and wide and although I thought it was back in style I couldn't help feeling like a character in "Guys and Dolls" singing…"I got the horse right here, his name is Paul Revere…"

I must tell you that the attention you receive at the post parade as an owner is rewarding. People shouting their good luck wishes, and others pulling you aside as if to get some dark inside information about the race. It's almost like Rocky walking to the ring protected by his trainers with his gloves raised on high, waving at the crowd.

Roger was a bit more careful in the paddock area this time. Oh, I forgot to tell you. Remember the last match race between Our Tsunami Su and Life's Not Easy? Ernie kept warning Roger to stand aside and give the horses room in the small paddock area as they paraded. Roger, who takes up quite a bit of room himself, didn't listen to Ernie and positioned himself quite close to the horses as they made the last turn at the back of the paddock.

As Life's Not Easy passed Roger, my partner leaned closer to the horse to get a real good look. Like two rockets fired off an F-16 fighter, the two rear legs of the horse shot out. Bang, whomp…right in the ass and across the paddock went Roger. The big fellow put his right hand behind him, bit his lip and disappeared down the entry hall to the pad-dock area. Getz's horse had sealed my partner's tush shut for a week.

So as we stood now in the paddock area, watching the parade and answering questions and accepting acco-lades, I couldn't help noticing the healthy distance Roger gave all of the horses.

Out came Ten Taylor Road into the sun. E.T. Baird was ready to prove that the crowd which had driven us up to 5-1 odds was sadly mistaken. Gee Can He Dance and Imperial Gold were the favorites. Most of the rest of the field was bunched up in the area of 4-1 or 5-1 except Run Em Over which was at an astronomical 55-1 odds.

I looked in the form at the horse Imperial Gold. For the life of me I couldn't figure why the crowd had given him second favored status. The horse had only won $19,890 life-time and had been unruly at the gate in his last race. I passed him off as an also ran.

This was the moment of truth. The bell rang, the gates opened and out came the seven contestants running for the largest prize I personally had ever been in a contest for.

I had become accustomed to seeing Ten Taylor Road leap into the lead. However, this was not to be. As the horses sprang from the gate, Imperial Gold went almost to its knees in front of Ten Taylor Road. E.T. had to pull in the gelding to prevent Ten Taylor Road from running over that turkey. At the same time, Danc'n Jake, taking advantage of the hole left by Ten Taylor's sudden stop, cut us off.

By the time the horses had recovered and run past the grandstands for the first time, Ten Taylor was in fifth place by a good 12 lengths with only Special Buck and the 55-1 shot behind him.

I could almost hear Ten Taylor mumbling about his bad luck at the start as he methodically attempted to make up ground on the field.

At the half he was in third and turning for home. I could hear Georgeff cry "and here comes Ten Taylor Road!" I peered through my binoculars and there was this gallant, rangy, black gelding pounding his way to the lead at the final pole.

Now I truly would like to hold this picture in my mind for a few seconds. For, at this point in time, I was less than three seconds from the realization of all of my dreams. This book was three seconds away from completion. I was about to own a "big horse."

However, the disruption at the start of the race was about to take its toll. The sound of pounding hoofs once again coming up to challenge Ten Taylor was apparent. The brave gelding, looked over his shoulder, as he had before, lowered his head and went deep into his gigantic heart for all that remained.

This time he came up empty, there was nothing left. Danc'n Jake flew by at the wire followed closely by Special Buck. Ten Taylor was third by four at the finish, three lengths ahead of his arch rival Gee Can He Dance. We had won the battle with the Gabriel mount and lost the war.

In my heart I know that if Imperial Gold had not gone to his knees at the start of the race, the yards we lost at the beginning would have made the difference. However, "if 'ifs' and 'buts' were Candy and Nuts, we would all have a merry Christmas."

We came in third, good for a little over $11,000.

The next day the four top horses, including Ten Taylor Road, were mentioned as contenders for the Illinois Derby. Third in a graded stake race is still something to be proud of, and besides, we were up to a little over $55,000 in winnings over the past two months. America is truly a "wonderful country."

*"Raising horses differs only from raising children in as much as when it comes to the patter of little feet there is twice the noise."*

CHAPTER **11**

# THE STABLE GROWS

On April 4, 1992 Paula and I experienced one of the most pleasant experiences in the horse business—our first birth.

Remember the mare in foal that Teri sold to me along with the filly weanling? Well, we were playing cards Saturday night when we received a call from Dave Noby at Horizon Farms. It was about 10:45 p.m. He told us that we had about 30 minutes to drive out to Barrington if we didn't want to miss the birth.

Paula and I jumped into our car and arrived at Horizon just as Moonlight Drive was delivering the foal. It was a filly. The foal was an identical twin to its mother. Both were bays with a crooked white streak down the nose.

Horizon Farm has a barn which they call their hospital and the farm employs midwives who foal some 60 to 80 horses a year. The gestation period of a horse is just over 11 months. The stall was dimly lit with a red bulb. There was an incredibly bad stench coming from a sterilizing solution. Moonlight Drive lay on her side with her tail braided and taped. The newborn foal was at her side.

The foal instantly attempted in vain to stand up. The

next 30 minutes were filled with attempts of the foal to stand. The mare paid some small attention to the little one, but in general seemed to be attempting to recover from the entire ordeal.

Paula put her finger in the foal's mouth. Without teeth the young horse was as gentle as a kitten. The foal responded with a natural sucking reflex.

At a point in time, some 45 minutes after birth, the foal rose to her wobbly feet and made her first attempt at nursing. The mare stood still as the suckling made a pass under her only to bang into the wall. We applauded her first successful connection to the mare.

Paula snapped photo after photo in hopes of capturing at least one treasure. The stench was getting to me as my lungs began to burn. It was getting late. Paula and I left Horizon, tired and elated, but with a new experience under our belts.

The next day we returned to find the mare and the suckling together in a small pen. The suckling was wearing a warming blanket. It looked just like a racehorse only in miniature. Only one day old and it was dancing and playing. It was hard to believe that yesterday it didn't exist.

Our first inclination was to name the horse Bang the Walls. Wouldn't you know it, after checking the computer I found that the name belonged to a 1989 foal.

We had already named a horse after my daughter Missy, so it was only right that we honored my son, Spin, with a namesake.

Paula and I put our heads together and came up with Out for a Spin. With the mare named Moonlight Drive, it was a natural.

The colt we had purchased was now a yearling. Motion Call, as we renamed him, found a home at Horizon Farm. During the months of February and March he was broken and then ridden daily.

Tim Koertgen is the trainer at Horizon who is responsible for the care and training of Motion Call. Tim is a very young 40. He looked like a kid, but had the insight and experience of a seasoned veteran.

Motion Call is doing everything expected of him. Two or three times a week, Paula and I ride out to Barrington and watch one of the staff jockeys ride him indoors around barn 10. A grandson of the great Secretariat, this colt was growing by leaps and bounds. He already stood almost 16 hands high and he was still a yearling.

I stare at him and think how incredible it will be when he leaps from the starting gate for the first time and we realize if we have been raising a champion or a dud. No one, not even Ernie, can tell if this horse has heart or will run until it actually runs. Some of the prettiest horses in the world just do not want to play the game.

During the past months many different types of setbacks have occurred with this colt. We scanned his knees and found that they are nowhere near closing. Oh, let me explain. In all mammals, the long bones continue to grow outward from a growth plate and only when the growing stops do the joints come together. In a racehorse, the knees usually close sometime in the second year. Some horses are slower at this than others. Such is the case with Motion Call.

I received a call one day from Dave Noby at Horizon telling me that Motion Call had come down with a strange infection caused by a protozoa. The medical term was

Equine Protozoa Melitis or EPM. The horse was quarantined and, after feeding it about $5 worth of drugs a day for a month and a half, was cured.

I know that all my hopes are on the hoofs of Ten Taylor Road for this year and I will have to be satisfied to just make friends with Motion Call and feed him carrots.

Actually, I must confess that I find a great deal of pleasure in coming out to the farm and watching the horses work out. I get to wear my cowboy boots and jeans and pretend that I am on the Ponderosa. I have spent many a pleasure-filled hour feeding the young horses and walking or riding the trails from barn to barn. This is a part of the horse business that is a real bonus. I really don't think that God subtracts time from a person's life while he is engaged in such an activity. The tranquillity is overpowering. This has become a new aphrodisiac.

Missy's Shystar, the filly weanling is just as independent as ever. We do not get to visit her very often, but Peggy sends us notes every month with the bill keeping us informed of her progress. I do not share any hopes and dreams for this filly. Whatever she provides us with will be accepted gratefully.

When we have seen her, she eats like a horse, (pun intended) gulping down carrot after carrot, without so much as stopping to breathe.

Missy costs us $5 per day and Motion Call $28 while in training. The suckling and the mare together cost $17 per day.

It is my intention to gift the mare to Julie DePinto's sister in New York when the foal is weaned. Until now, these young horses are costing me $50 per day without any income. I have assigned a book value to each horse on the basis of their cost, but in this market I have no hopes of recovering my outlay unless they can run.

My stable is growing. I now realize that I am committed financially to a very expensive business and for the first time I am experiencing the nervousness associated with the perils of the trade.

*"If you can't win them all, then you're going to lose some."*

CHAPTER **12**

# TAYLOR ROAD
# STAKES DROPPER

Right after the Nash I asked Ernie if we were going into the Illinois Derby. The race was to be held on May 9 and since we were nominated and had won the Lost Code and had come in third in the Nash we were almost a certainty to make the field.

Ernie was rather evasive and for the first time I started hearing things about Ten Taylor looking a bit thin and his right ankle looking swollen after the race on the 18th.

Truthfully, both Roger and I wanted to be in the Derby more than anything in the world. We begged Ernie to accept the nomination. Everyday the racing news came out with speculations about who the nominations would be and we were always mentioned. "Local hero Ten Taylor Road, winner of the Lost Code Breeders' Cup Stakes and third in the Nash..." was the way we were most often referred to.

Ernie had stuck his neck out to the media and painted himself into a corner saying that the Illinois Derby was next. However, I could tell from his comments that he was not thinking Derby.

Somewhere around the last week in April, Ernie got sicker than a dog. His blood sugar shot way up and you could tell the way he was breathing and coughing that he was in trouble.

We met him in his little office at Sportsman's the morning that he went into the hospital. He and his wife Dee were making arrangements for the yearly move to Arlington. The season was winding down at Sportsman's and although Ernie looked and felt like shit, he had a million things to do.

On top of it, Roger and I kept after him about the Derby.

Finally, at that meeting, Ernie said, "Da race is coming up too tough." He explained to us that Ten Taylor Road is a young gelding with a lot of heart and if he goes in over his head at this stage of the game we could ruin him. Now, to tell you the truth, this made no sense to Roger and I. Gee Can He Dance was in the race as well as Special Buck and Danc'n Jake and we had run damn good against them before. Besides, these horses are all 3-year olds and Double T's had been running against some of the best of them all of his racing career.

Ernie stood his ground. This was to be our first owner-trainer disagreement. Roger and I went into a pow-wow and after we refused to budge, Ernie agreed to leave him in the race. Roger and I had reservations about the validity of our veto over his decision. What if the horse came up hurt?

Ernie said that if we gave up the Derby he could promise us a good race and said, in time, if we had patience, that we would not be disappointed.

Ernie called us the next day from his hospital bed and told us that there was a stakes race named the Prince Forli Purse being run the same day as the Derby for $30,000 and we could get in.

Roger and I still did not want to give up the idea of being in the Derby, but consoled ourselves with the thought of the $20,000 first prize, available in the Prince Forli.

Tuesday, May 5, was four days after the running of the Kentucky Derby. The owner of a 3-year old horse gets the same feeling as a boy who turns 14 and knows that he will never again play little league baseball. Is there life after the Kentucky Derby? We were still in the Illinois Derby. Then the call came from Troy. Double T's had come down with a case of the colic. We were out of the Illinois Derby, we were out of the Prince Forli. The headlines now read, "TEN TAYLOR ROAD STAKES DROPPER." They might just as well have read, "LEE FORMAN FLUNKS OUT OF COLLEGE."

I began to visit Ten Taylor every day after that call. Truthfully, I couldn't see anything wrong with him and I almost accused Ernie and his veterinarian, Dick Hume, of bullshitting us. I figured that this was Ernie's way of winning the standoff between him and Roger and me. It made no sense that he would go to this extent just to withdraw from a race. I was content to believe that we had just been kicked in the ass by bad racing luck.

Ernie moved back into Arlington Park that next Sunday. I had never had a horse stabled here and the excitement of getting my license changed over to Arlington and receiving my passes and auto identification was overwhelming. Ten Taylor had an excellent workout that morning.

Ernie drove me to the workout in his beat up old electric golf cart. I made the criminal mistake of putting my foot on the dashboard of that piece of crap and Ernie went crazy. I quickly removed my foot and apologized.

As we drove up to the track, other trainers, clockers, owners, racetrack employees and jockeys greeted Ernie. It was like driving through the streets with the King of England. And to think, I had put my foot on his throne.

After the workout Ernie drove me back and said that if the horse was not sore that he would be entered the next Sunday in a non-winners of two allowance race for $18,000.

I was excited to be in a race at Arlington, but the letdown from being eliminated from the Derby and the Prince Forli would not be soothed by an entry into an allowance race.

Now the papers read, "Talk about an easy spot. If this gelding runs the way he has in his five previous efforts this season he should wipe out this field."

I looked at the other horses in the field. They were all older horses. They had competed with the likes of Tory Sound and Katahaula County and King Turk. Their speed would be faster than the 3-year olds competing in the Derby. This has to be bullshit. How could the derby be too tough and this race be a piece of cake?

At race time we were the overwhelming favorite at 3-5. All the sports writers had the race as a piece of cake for Double T's. He was everybody's best bet of the day. Everybody but John Brokopp. I have been following Mr. Brokopp's selections and it seems that he waits until everybody else goes right before he decides to go left.

The bell sounded, the gates opened, and the older, faster, and stronger 4- and 5-year olds sprung forward. Ten Taylor seemed complacent, almost cocky, as he leisurely left the gate and found a spot three lengths off the lead.

Ten Taylor Road had run both shorter and longer races before but never 6 1/2 furlongs. We had expected a wire-to-wire lead. At the second call, E.T. Baird looked for racing room, picked a spot and took the lead. Rare Silence, a 4-year old gelding by Silent Screen, took up the chase and made a match race out of it to the wire. Ten Taylor Road taunted the 4-year old with his talent. It was all Ten Taylor Road. He had disappointed no one except John Brokopp. Ten Taylor had knocked off the 6 1/2 furlongs in 1:18 flat.

We drove back to the barn to visit our horse after the race. I took several pictures of the horse with my nephew Tom Baer. For Tommy, this race will live in his memory as one of his most exciting events.

I must mention that we are by this time pros at taking photos in the winners circle. I don't think the thrill will ever wear off. However, we are more cognizant of what is happening around us now as the photos are being taken. Julie and Vito were at the race and participated in the photo as well as Tommy. Roger and Dawn had their children and several nieces and nephews. I searched the background in the photo and for the first time I could not find Bobby Baird.

When I bumped into Bobby the next week he told me that with such a crowd, he kept jumping up to get into the photo but the crowd was too tall and too wide. This photo will go down in history as being the only win of E.T.'s without his father in the picture.

This win put an additional $10,800 in Ten Taylor Road's till. The betting Roger and I did was minimal. The perfecta was a mere $13.80.

It was now the beginning of June. There are small signals that you are making it in every industry. When a horse has his workouts printed separately in the Daily Racing Form you know that special attention is being paid to that horse. On this date, Ten Taylor's rather impressive mile workout was printed in a separate section of the news with split times.

Ernie called and said he was a little concerned about Ten Taylor's front right ankle. It had come up hot after the work but he had been able to cool it down with a chemical agent. Ernie had entered the horse in the Ridan Handicap, an overnight handicap. The purse was $27,000 and the competition would be pretty stiff.

I wish you could all see this. Every sports writer picks us second or third except one turkey. Guess who? Correct. John Brokopp has us right on top in big black letters.

This was a beautiful day. Especially beautiful because my daughter has finally made a token appearance at a race. Until this time she has been at school, busy with finals and applying for a regular job. I can't fault her for not being here before. Winning this race was more important today because I wanted to honor her with a photo in the winner's circle at Arlington.

The bettors had us at 6-1, a rather casual betting stance to take with such an impressive winner. I'll bet they had us higher, and Roger and I alone lowered the odds by pounding the windows with hundreds.

I must admit that the field was quite impressive. Each of the entries had won some $40,000 to $60,000 and each boasted of impressive wins over other such horses. I still felt like a stakes dropper. The bloom was off the rose and this was just another race. Ernie kept mumbling about the horse's ankle as we positioned ourselves in the grand-stands to watch the race.

I will not glorify our third place finish with a gate to finish line call. At the wire, a sore and tired Ten Taylor Road was passed by Special Buck and Held Accountable. Three thousand dollars in prize money and a sore gelding is what we left the track with that day.

Little did I know that I was about to add to my horse racing vocabulary such terms as green osselet, liver enzyme imbalance and veterinarian bills.

*"An apple a day cost me an apple tree."*

CHAPTER **13**

# ENTER VET,
# EXIT SEASON

I am told by those who have been in this game for a life-time, that this is the hard part. We are going to have to sit back and watch for a while as we wait for our horse to heal.

Within a few days after that last race, I met with Ernie, Troy and Dick Hume. The consensus was that Ten Taylor Road had several problems that had to be solved before we went on with him.

First of all, his right ankle was becoming swollen and hot after races and workouts and filling with fluid. Secondly, the horse was looking rank and was not eating properly.

Hume made the decision to rest him for three weeks, ice his ankles and change his feed. In the meantime a blood chemistry would be taken and Ten Taylor would be wormed.

By July 1, Taylor Road had lost about 75 pounds, his ankle was not responding to the ice packs and we met again with Dick Hume.

The blood chemistry detected a liver enzyme problem and the x-ray of his front right ankle showed a green osselet.

Now I was certain that my horse was not an alcoholic, how could he have a liver problem? The veterinarian answered me with a straight answer, "I do not have a clue."

Hume did say that there was a medication which could cure the problem and we would start on it immediately. In reference to the osselet he was more specific.

The bone between the ankle is cushioned by soft cartilage. When an osselet forms it is similar to a heel spur on a human. It is at first a soft infection which later takes the place of the cartilage. The term "green" means that it has just started and that we had an excellent chance of burning the infection out and creating a new blood supply to the area to prevent its recurrence.

The process by which this is done is called pin firing. A hot metal object which looks like a soldering iron is placed into the ankle in about 50 spots. This creates an acute condition onto which a blistering agent is later applied. When the pin firing blisters off the ankle and heals, hopefully, the osselet will be gone and a new blood supply will appear and prevent its reoccurrence.

I asked Dick how long this process would take. He said he has had horses return to the track within 90 days of pin firing. This was comforting as I really wanted to race again at Arlington before the season ended in October. I consented to the treatment.

Ten Taylor was moved to Horizon Farm and the medication and pin firing was started. Paula and I made a regular visit twice a week to brush him and feed him carrots. At the same time we were able to watch Motion Call recover from his protozoa infection and begin to work out lightly.

It was like having a grandmother in a nursing home.

Everybody else was at the track with their horses and we were feeding carrots to sick puppies.

I began to meet people at the farm who were undergoing similar problems. The same conversations were played over and over. I should have brought a program with his track record and saved myself a lot of wind. It was always what could have been and what might be.

If you are going to ever consider being part of this game, get prepared for this type of situation. I have a $3,000 a month outlay and no foreseeable source of income. The value of my stock is at an all time low. I am told that if I do not have the balls to withstand this type of fire, then get out of the kitchen now.

I refused to quit. I have set out to complete a task and damn, baring bankruptcy or illness, I am going to see this through. I am also not going to make a common mistake in the business.

Some people just have to have constant action. Roger is like that. He has 10 trotters and even if six of them are broken down he can race four a week. Some people would go out and claim another horse right now and try to get an income earner.

I am not going to fall into that trap. I am going to do everything I can to help this horse get back to the track and I am not going to add to my monthly burden. The people who do that sour quickly on the game. I have a friend, Lonnie, who, every time he sees me says, "are you broke yet?"

I had begun a regular ritual. I golf Saturday morning and spend the afternoon with my horses. Roger calls me from time to time and asks how the horse is doing. I check in with Ernie, mostly to get a tip on whatever he has running that day.

Ten Taylor eventually entered the blistering stage. Fortunately, his liver problem had resolved itself and he had begun to eat again. In fact he is taking on quite a belly. It's going to take a lot of working off when he returns to the track.

I met with Dick Hume again. More bad news. Motion Call's knees are still not closed and Ten Taylor Road will need at least until the beginning of the year to heal. It's time for patience. I can return to golf and handicapping and close this book until something more interesting than feeding carrots happens.

*"Only once did I know a dog that got hoarse...I now know a lot of horses that became dogs."*

CHAPTER **14**

# TEN TAYLOR SWIMS
# THE DOG PADDLE

The summer had turned to fall and the fall to winter. It was the last Sunday in November. Out for a Spin, the weanling, was still at Regal Creek, in Harvard. Missy's Shystar was now at Horizon being broken and Motion Call was on his way down to the Fair Grounds in New Orleans to complete his training. It is our hope to have Motion Call back in Chicago in time for the opening of Sportsman's Park on February 15th.

A strange twist of fate had occurred which is worth mentioning. During Ten Taylor's 1992 campaign, his arch rival was a handsome chestnut named Gee Can He Dance, trained by Leo and Betty Gabriel. Gee Can He Dance always reminded me of my Motion Call. They were the same color, both with blond manes. They both were large and powerful looking horses and both stood out in a crowd.

I am still very fond of Ernie who has had a decent season at Hawthorne. I think we both have earned a great deal of each others respect. Trainers are very busy people and sometimes the owner is overlooked in the planning stages of a horse's career. Ernie now includes me in his every thought about my horses. I have become his attorney and feel confident that we have established a firm relationship. I defend Ernie to other jealous owners and trainers who have less than favorable comments about my friend.

Ernie called for Motion Call to be sent to him at Hawthorne to complete his training. I called Ernie and we discussed the situation. The tracks are closed between December 31 and February 15, and the only way Ernie earns a buck is by training during the off-season. Personally, I would like to see this wonderful man take some time off himself and come back fresh, but he seems to be one minded and will plod on through the final bell.

Ernie, asked me to have Motion call stay here in Chicago over the winter. I refused. Even though I know that it was like taking $45 a day out of his pocket, I had to make the decision which I believed was in my best interest. I opted to send Motion Call to a warm climate.

I asked Tim Koertgen from Horizon Farms who and where he would recommend. Tim told me that he had two other horses going down to Louisiana with a local trainer for January and February and that the Fair Grounds had a perfect surface during the winter and the weather is conducive to training.

Tim says that this trainer has one spot left. I jumped at the chance and said a conditional, yes. Who is the trainer? Wouldn't you know it, Lou and Betty Gabriel.

I called them and discussed the training of Motion Call. You would think that the rivalry created by our other two horses would prevent this type of relationship from existing.

Both Betty and Lou were thrilled to take Motion Call and notwithstanding the fact that I would soon be running him against their horses, I am confident that they will do everything in their power to create a champion. This is something pretty special that exists in this game and no other. It is a common love of the sport which transcends rivalry.

Naturally, I called Ernie and discussed my decision with him. If I had given the horse to Charlie Bettis I would have lost a friend, trainer and client in one second. Betty and Lou were good friends of Ernie and knowing that I wanted it, he gave up his financial interest and consented.

Meanwhile, Ten Taylor Road was transferred to a place called Farmington Green. The Green was a farm owned and operated by two brothers, Carmen and Mat Carfi. Mat Carfi was, coincidentally, partners with Marlene Silver in a great 5-year old named Tory Sound. Marlene is the wife of Earl Silver, my high school pal who owned Silken Road, the horse Ten Taylor hockey-checked in his first race in Chicago.

We were quite impressed during our first visit to Farmington Green. Carmen led us around and displayed the neatly-kept barns and stalls and we were in awe at the value of the animals which were laid up there for training and conditioning.

We were then introduced to the pool for the first time. Ten Taylor Road would be using swimming as a means of returning to the track. His ankles were healed and neatly sculptured. However, he was out of condition and needed a way to return to training without pounding on those ankles.

Swimming would be used to increase his stamina and tighten up his body. He would regain his wind without a chance of injuring his ankle. The other alternative would be to run him at Hawthorne on a track which would soon be inundated with snow, ice and melting agents.

The pool was 40 feet long with a 17 degree incline at its entrance and 15 degree incline at its exit. The pool was 8 foot wide and 12 feet deep in the middle. Multiple whirlpool jets were pointed at the animal causing a resistance during swimming. The water was heated to 80 degrees and purified.

I am not going to vouch for the cleanliness of the pool as I am told that quite a few steeds poop on the way in and poop on the way out.

The horse's tail is braided and a rope is hooked to it. As the horse is led into the pool the rope is extended until the horse is in the deep part of the pool. The rope is tied off and the horses head is kept secure by two lead ropes held by grooms.

Ten Taylor would be led through a couple of times without swimming and then attempt a one minute swim. After the swim, his pulse will be noted as well as the time it takes for his breathing to return to normal. If the horse is in condition to do so, he will be advanced 15 seconds per day until he is able to swim for nine minutes.

A nine minute swim is the equivalent of a three mile gallop. Carmen has designed this pool differently from his competition. Most pools are circular and the horse only develops on one side at a time.

The horse in a circular pool can fake it and dog paddle with his front legs only. The long pool forces the animal to swim with all fours equally and to put forth the effort or sink.

During Double T's first swim I asked Carmen how he knows if a horse has had enough. Carmen said, "I look at their eyes. When a horse has had it, he starts looking around for help."

Mid December was approaching and Paula and I were about to leave for a warm climate for the winter holidays. Ten Taylor Road was up to four and a half minutes of swimming a day. His ability to withstand the workout was outstanding. His body was sleek, black, and he again had that rank look of a greyhound. He was eating like a horse, (I couldn't resist that again). If there is a God of horses I only ask that his heart still be sound and that his will to win still be alive. I can smell the return of my champion.

I have returned to the OTBs as my only form of entertainment. Today is a very special day. Phillip Georgeff will retire today. Phil has been the voice of Chicago horse racing for 34 years. He has managed to call 96,000 races in his own unique style.

The racing program carried a history of Phil's career and one interesting fact leaped off the page. My middle name is Phillip and Phillip in Greek means, "lover of horses." I immediately felt that I was meant for this quest.

Right after New Years I checked in with Horizon. Missy's Shystar has been successfully broken. She is about to be returned to Regal Creek to be a horse again until the end of spring. I had bet Tim Koertgen that she would not be easy to break and would be an unwilling student. I am shocked to learn that she did everything expected of her and ran through the breaking without a whimper.

Lou Gabriel called from New Orleans. They put a tattoo on Motion Call's upper lip to identify him. They clipped his winter coat of hair and he is galloping every day. By February 1 they will X-ray his knees to see if they have

closed and breeze him for the first time.

Right now they are gate training him. Gate school is a very interesting part of the training of a young racehorse.

For the first few days the horse is led through the starting gate without stopping before doing his morning gallop.

Then the horse is asked to pause in the gate for a few attempts. After that the gate is closed when the horse pauses.

If the horse passes these tests then an attempt is made to walk the horse into the gate, close it and open it and walk the horse out. Next the horse is run out and finally the horse learns to leap out of the gate to the sound of the bell and opening of the gates.

I am told by Lou that the Fair Grounds has training races and after a horse has passed gate school and is physically ready to run he will compete in a few of them.

Meanwhile, Ten Taylor Road has completed a total physical. He was found to be in perfect shape with the exception of being low in certain electrolytes. This problem was being solved through diet.

He was swimming every day and was up to six minutes each time. This was like running two miles a day. Ernie will bring him back to Sportsman's Park about the first of February to gallop and then to breeze him. If he stays sound we should have an excellent chance of making some serious money at the opening of Sportsman's. Most of our competition will either be out of town or out of condition when the meet starts.

My parents tell me that it has not stopped raining in southern California. People may think that this is very bad, but I believe it may be a stroke of luck. With all of the flood-

ing out there, I can send Ten Taylor Road out to Santa Anita. I hear they have a dog paddle race at half a furlong for 3-year olds and up.

That might be the only way I will win a race this month. My pride and joy, my hope for Illinois's next "big horse" was swimming up to seven minutes a day in Carmen's pool.

I received a call from Betty Gabriel. She started off by telling me that she and Leo have successfully gate trained Motion Call and that he has been galloping every day. However, he has grown a full hand since reaching New Orleans and he is the largest horse Betty has seen in years at that young age. She doesn't know when he will stop growing. Anyway, he is too large for his age and she believes that going on with him now may injure his underdeveloped legs and ankles. She informed me that she and Leo believe it would be in our best interests to return him to Chicago to be turned out for a few months to allow him a chance to stop growing.

Well, I have been searching for a "big horse" figuratively speaking. Now I have one literally. I think we may have fed him one too many carrots. He is well over 16 1/2 hands high now and still going. I imagine by the time he gets into a race he will have to duck to get into the starting gate. If nothing else, he will certainly intimidate a lot of maidens in his first race, whenever that is.

This was another factor which put a great deal of importance on Ten Taylor's ability to return to winning form quickly. I had already suffered through seven months without a purse and I can tell you now that I was hurting.

The end of March came sooner than expected. I only

wish I could convey my frustrations to you. I brought Motion Call back to Illinois and sent him over to Regal Creek farm to wait for his knees to close. About the first of March, Geoff called and told me that they had X-rayed his legs and he was ready to start training. I sent him over to Ernie at $45 per day, and by this time all I can get out of Troy is that the horse is galloping every day and "he'll tell us when he is ready to breeze."

I wonder what he means by "he'll tell us." The horse will wake up one morning and yell, "Hey Ernie, I feel like breezing today." Give me a break!

In the meantime, Ten Taylor Road has had six good workouts and I am certain that the problem with his ankle is solved. The last few works were not as good as the first few in terms of the attempt that the horse made to run. When a horse runs casually it is said that "he is not taking the bit." You can tell when an animal is not trying his hardest.

Troy sent his blood for testing and again it came up short on hematocrit and hemoglobin, and further, the red count was low. In human's, that would indicate bleeding. In horses it indicates that the animal is training too hard and it is a good time to back off training and elevate the red cells. A normal volume of red cells is necessary to carry oxygen to the muscles and a reduced count means less oxygen and a decrease in performance. Dick Hume gave him a series of shots, and the last I heard, the blood was still reading a little on the low side but almost normal. Ten Taylor will be breezed as soon as his count has stabilized and he will run as soon as he takes the bit again in training.

In anticipation of Motion Call running his first race I ordered a new racing silk to represent the Forman family.

The silk that represented the partnership between the Forman and Samson families is gold with a black circle around a black F-S. I wanted the new silk to keep the same gold color so I added black and gold diamonds to the sleeves and created a logo out of two crossed gavels with an eight ball below them. My initials L.P.F. were spaced between the gavels. I became interested in finding out the history of racing silks so I took the liberty of researching their etiology. The Daily Racing Form publishes informational fillers which I read and took the liberty of duplicating here.

Individual racing silks were introduced in October, 1762 at Newmarket, England, when the then unique idea was conceived at a meeting of The Jockey Club. In the quaint phraseology of the time, it was decided that "For the greater convenience of distinguishing the horses in running, and also for the prevention of disputes arising from not knowing the colors of each rider the under-mentioned gentlemen have come to the resolution and agreement of having the colors annexed to the following names worn by their respective riders: The stewards therefore hope, in the name of The Jockey Club, that the named gentlemen will take care that the riders be provided with dresses accordingly."

Nineteen owners were listed: seven Dukes, one Marquis, four Earls, one Viscount, one Lord, two Baronets and three commoners.

The Duke of Cumberland chose "purple"; the Duke of Grafton, "sky blue"; the Duke of Devonshire, "straw"; the Duke of Northumberland, "yellow"; the Duke of Kingston, "crimson"; the Duke of Ancaster, "buff"; the Duke of Bridgewater, "garter blue"; and the Marquis of Rockingham, "green."

The Earl of Waldengrave selected "deep red"; the Earl of Oxford, "purple and white"; the Earl of March, "white"; the Earl of Gower, "blue"; Viscount Bolingbroke, "black"; Lord Grosvenor, "orange"; Sir John Moore, "darkest green"; Sir James Lowther, "orange"; Mr. R. Vernon, "an off white" the honorable Mr. Gereville, "brown trimmed with yellow"; and Mr. Jenison Shafto, "pink."

Originally, a black velvet huntsman's cap was the only type used by the riders and was more or less associated with the colors listed above, but this gave way to caps varied in color as we know them today.

The "straw" registered by the Duke of Devonshire is still used by the family and must be considered the oldest racing colors in existence. In 1787 the Lord Derby of that period changed his colors from green and white stripes to the famous "black with white cap" which we know today, and in 1799 the Grosvenor family colors were altered to "yellow, black cap" and have been used by the Dukes of Westminister ever since.[1]

God only knows if some historian, centuries from now, will list my gold and black in some treatise.

---

[1] The above history of racing silks was reprinted by permission of The Daily Racing Form.

*"Into each life a little rain must fall."*
*"I understand that, but today was really shit."*

CHAPTER **15**

# THE HARDEST
# LESSON OF ALL

Spring brought hope eternal that Ten Taylor would return and Motion Call would carry my gold and black colors to victory. Double T's breezed once a week for two months and each time I would ask Ernie if he was ready. Again and again he would say, "just one more good workout." I kept remembering that it was Ernie who said, "they don't pay for workouts." With Motion Call and Ten Taylor both at the track I was being hit for a fortune every month without a return.

When Ernie called and told me that Ten Taylor Road would run on April 14 in the featured eighth race at Sportsman's Park, I almost went into a hooting and hollering war dance. Just think, Motion Call was starting to breeze and Ten Taylor would be running in three days.

Tax day. The papers were full of stories again about the return of Ten Taylor Road. The "On The Track" column boasted a headline, "Taylor Road vs. Inca Trail." The Green Sheet and all the handicappers had us as the best bet of the day. Ten Taylor went off at 8-5. I was expecting C.H. Marquez to be riding Ten Taylor because Ernie and I had met with his agent and agreed upon it. Ernie had a run-in with E.T. Baird's father Bobby and didn't want E.T. to ride for him anymore. It seems that Roger and I have no control over the situation and so we went with the flow.

However, the day of the race we were surprised to find out that Ray Sibille was riding our horse. Ray had been a great rider in the past and was now making a comeback; and, had we agreed upon him, I suppose Roger and I would not have been so upset. Ernie had put Marquez on a horse named Zopilote and had entered both horses in the same race. I confronted Ernie with this and he grunted the same shit when asked if Our Tsunami Su was sound. It's not English but it sounds like, "tsssso...kay." That, plus a wave of the hand in your face by Ernie, was supposed to clear up any problems. Now I dare you to take my place and try to tell Ernie to pull another horse out of the race or trade jockeys. It wasn't to be.

The race was not monumental. Zopilote came out of the gate like a bullet and died like a pig at the half mile marker. Ten Taylor was ridden like a piece of valuable china and not prodded or hit by Sibille. He came out of the gate fourth and ran fourth. Ernie applauded his efforts and told us we had just been paid $1,700 for a great workout and that in a few weeks the cash would start rolling in.

Ernie had told me that we should be looking for another six furlong event so as not to tire Ten Taylor Road out in longer races. A few weeks passed and no races appeared for the horse. I stopped by Sportsman's Park and picked up a condition book (a diary of the upcoming races.) I leafed through it until I saw a race on Saturday May 1, which was for three and up, non-winners of three other than maiden or claiming. Perfect, two weeks apart and six furlongs.

When I called Ernie, I knew that he wasn't being honest with me. I told him about the race and he said. "Too short, we need a mile so he can rest" and "We found lead in his hair, must be from the water here, it's slowing him down" and "the doctor thinks his blood is still too low." I finally got Ernie to admit that he had just entered into the same May 1 race with a certain horse I shall call "The Ghost," who was a 3-year old that had just won the Lost Code Breeders' Cup Stakes. I don't think that Ernie wanted these two speedsters running against each other from the same barn as they were quite capable of hooking up in a speed duel and killing each other while another horse came from off the pace and ran off with the race.

The next series of events which took place will remain in my memory forever. I threw a fit with Ernie. I told him that he was not being honest with Roger and me and that I was probably wasting a lot of time and money on Motion Call by leaving him with Ernie.

I called Horizon Farms and told Dave Noby to pick up Motion Call immediately, partly as a money-saving measure and partly as a power play with Ernie. It didn't take Ernie too long to catch on. Before you knew it, we were entered into the same race on May 1st with The Ghost, and Dave Noby was on the phone telling me that he wouldn't have room for Motion Call for at least another two weeks.

Ernie does not let a lot of grass grow under his feet. He knows just how to manipulate people and animals for his best interests. This time, however, the results of our power struggle had a fatal ending. Ten Taylor was again ridden by Sibille and Marquez was on The Ghost. Before the race, I cornered Ray and told him that I really needed this one. I told him to take the horse out to the lead and press The Ghost and even hook up with him if necessary.

Ernie denies it, but he told Ray to rate Ten Taylor and not to hook up with the speed. Ernie figured that The Ghost, if given an easy lead, would walk away with a win easily and that Roger and I would be satisfied with a second or third coming from off the pace.

Ten Taylor Road was in unfamiliar territory when checked up out of the gate by Sibille. He settled into an uncomfortable seventh place where mud was kicked up into his face. Ray asked the horse to respond coming out of the turn but the confused gelding did everything he could to prevent himself from being stoned by the shit being thrown in his face by the speed. When the race ended, this proud title holder was seventh in a seven horse contest. The Ghost lost to a 25-1 shot, Glass Town. But Ernie got his way.

Well, you say, that doesn't sound like a fatal consequence to me. Here is the irony of the totality of events. Motion Call stayed at Sportsman's with Ernie and was scheduled for another 3/8ths of a mile breeze on Wednesday May 5.

I truly did not sleep a wink Tuesday night. I kept thinking we were just plain "fucked" in that last race and that at least we could look forward to boxcar odds in the next race at Arlington. Further, this would be one of Motion Calls first attempts at a full breeze and maybe, just maybe, he would turn in a burner which would convince both Ernie and I that he was ready to run. In my dreams, I pictured him winning a race with Pat Day on his back and then turning to the crowd and rising up on his back legs like Silver did at the end of the Lone Ranger movies, Pat would wave his whip at the crowd and Motion Call would give out a loud whinny.

I arrived at Sportsman's a full hour early in anticipation of what could be one of the proudest moments of my racing career. Almost like a father watching his son learn to ride a bike or catch a football. I spent about a half an hour running my fingers through his mane and tickling his nose. He kept prodding me for carrots which I knew were a no-no before a breeze or a race. I looked into his eyes and we shared my dreams together.

Soon he was led out to the track and before I could climb up on the boards which would allow me to see over the track fence, he was out of sight. Ernie nudged me, "Here he comes" and as he pointed, my proud steed, golden mane flying in the morning air, flew by us. I picked him up in the glasses about two furlongs from the finish line and just as suddenly as I picked him up he disappeared. I dropped the binoculars and slid my own glasses back on my nose in time to see the jockey dismount and watch Motion Call, in pain, raising his right hind leg. Another jock who had been riding next to him at the time rode up to Ernie and me at the fence and shouted, "It's broke." All I could think of is that they shoot horses, don't they? In no time the ambulance brought him back in front of the Poulos barn. I entered the van just after the track vet.

There stood Motion Call on three legs. Not a whimper. Like a proud champion, too noble to cry out in pain. I stroked his forehead as I had only moments before as I saw him shiver and shake in fear, and watched as clouds of steam rose from his sweat drenched body. I looked into the same eyes that had just moments before shared my dreams and all I could see now was fear. A small tear formed and rolled down his nose. I wiped it gently away with the sleeve of my coat.

The vet looked up and shook his head. He drew a small picture of the break in the cannon bone, which for my proud gelding was a death warrant. I shared one small brief moment more with the horse who would bear my colors no longer and I turned to the vet and Dee Poulos and said with my head lowered, and in a whisper, "do whatever is necessary."

The very same tears flow now as I put down these words. In the album in which I kept his photos, hoping that some day they would hold the same proud headlines that Ten Taylor Road accumulated, I wrote..."IN FOND MEMORY OF A BRAVE BIG HORSE" "Motion Call was put down at Sportsman's Park this 5th day of May 1993 after suffering a multiple fracture of the cannon bone of the right hind leg during a workout at 9 a.m." I had at last learned a very hard but necessary lesson about horse racing at the cost of the life of a good friend. I shall never allow myself to become this attached to an animal again. "Into each life a little rain must fall...today was really shit!"

*"So many people want to buy my horse that
no one will make an offer."*

CHAPTER **16**

# BIG HORSE
# GOES A CLAIMING

Ernie had always said, "Run out your conditions first."
That meant that we should keep trying to run Ten
Taylor in non-winners of three other than maiden or claiming. The next race in the condition book was scheduled for
May 12.

This was a seven furlong race and we had pulled the
rail. I threw a fit with Ernie about Sibille's ride against The
Ghost and told him that I would call Bobby Baird myself
and that E.T. would again be given a chance on double T's.

Ernie didn't even show up in the paddock area. I
gave a leg up to E.T. and told him to get the front and stay
there. I am afraid he listened too well. The wind was blowing up the backstretch and right into the face of the horses
at the finish line. Ten Taylor came right out with blazing
fractions and at three quarters a host of numbers led by
Mark Guidry on Captain Butler came flying by him at the
finish line. E.T. said he almost got knocked off the horse by
the wind as they passed him. I watched the replay twice
before I conceded that we had again come away without a
purse.

We decided to keep trying at the same level, so on May 21 we came right back in the same allowance level and at the same distance. Again E.T. set incredible fractions of :22 1/5, :45 1/5 and 1:10 1/5 before Ten Taylor died at the finish line again without a purse. The trouble is that E.T. was not giving the horse a breather. There was so much speed in these races that we were being pressed the whole way setting up the race for the closer. The horses we were losing to were not chopped liver and would go on to stakes races and multiple wins. However, the bills at the end of the month kept coming and to date he had managed to win only $1,656 since he began his 1993 campaign.

Ernie suggested dropping him to a claiming race. I took the suggestion with the same degree of acceptability as someone asking to share my wife with me. The thought of putting a tag on my "Big Horse" was too much for me to handle.

We came right back on June 16 into a shorter allowance race at 6 1/2 furlongs. Ernie had told me that he wouldn't tolerate E.T. going back up on the horse and that giving Ray Sibille, a more experienced jockey, another chance was the right move.

Again, we were either overmatched or Sibille was not the answer. Ray rated the horse third for most of the race but Ten Taylor Road would not respond to the call at the finish, and Sibille backed off the whip at the finish line to let two horses steal third and fourth. We came out of the race with a paltry $600. I approached Sibille after the race to find out what had occurred and as I opened my mouth to speak, the experienced jockey said, "Why don't you run this nag down at 25 where he belongs." I was so flabbergasted that I stood there in the tunnel leading away from the track with my mouth open collecting dust. Run Ten Taylor Road, son of Kennedy Road in a claiming race? Not on your fucking life. "Hey!" I yelled at him walking away in the distance, "You'll never ride another one of my horses again!"

My meeting with Ernie that next Sunday was a beauty. Ernie, Dee, Roger and another of Ernie's owners, whom I shall refer to from here on as "Dick," were all there, all with one common purpose—to convince me to run Ten Taylor in a claiming race. Dick and Roger kept saying, "The worst that can happen is that you make ten g's in the purse, another three betting, and pick up twenty five on the claim. You can buy a lot of horse for $38,000." Dee and Ernie were more tactful and kept explaining that very few horses are claimed and who would take a chance with a winless horse who had not yet made a comeback from an injury? "O.K." was all I could manage. The word stuck in my throat as though I had just condemned my best friend to death. Ten Taylor Road would run in the next available six furlong, $25,000 claimer.

Agreeing to run was easier than getting a race. As each twenty-five thousand short race came up in the condition book it was set aside for a lack of entries. Finally on June 27, a Sunday, we drew into a six furlong event for a purse of $15,000. We even drew our lucky number 5 post. I had asked Ernie to get me Wiggy Ramos as a jockey. Wiggy had already committed to ride for Joe Broussard on a horse named Mutah. Ernie said he would like to give another veteran a chance and go with Earlie Fires.

We went to the post the 3-1 choice behind Mutah. Ernie told Earlie to save some horse. Earlie parked Ten

Taylor third behind the speed, Prince Compliance and Mac Attack. On the turn he began to fly past the leaders. Behind him was a horse named Mission Highland. Paula had seen Mission Highland in the paddock and remarked at how crooked the horse was and how he was bandaged from head to toe and that the rider, Cowboy Jones, looked like he was 60. As Earlie began to make his move past the speed, he moved Ten Taylor wide so as to let Mission Highland and Cowboy Jones through. A photo at the finish found us a bridesmaid to the crooked horse and elderly rider. I was surrounded by angry bettors and friends who were certain that Cowboy had been given the race. I was satisfied with Fires ride and furthermore, the $3,000 purse together with the sight of watching my own stable leading my horse away from a claiming race was such a relief that the thought of any wrongdoing never entered my mind.

"We gonna do it again," was Ernie's comment on the race, "and next time we gonna win." I had not agreed to continue to run my horse in claimers, but when the next race popped up on July 7 and Ernie drew in with Fires on board, I took a deep breath and again watched as my precious steed set out of the gate with tag on his head. This time we came out of the gate first. Ten Taylor had a look of determination on him as he sped to the lead. Fires checked him up and dropped back to sixth. Shades of Mark Guidry. What in the hell was this speed horse doing rating again? Coming out of the turn Ten Taylor made his big move. Sixth, fifth then fourth. Earlie tried to change leads and the horse lugged out and lost ground. Again Fires went to the whip and again Ten Taylor responded poorly. The leaders were eating up ground as the black gelding straightened out and came charging. At the finish line we had run third, only a length off the leaders. Another big attempt by the horse, another excuse by the jock, and $1,650 more in the till.

I kept calling Ernie but he wouldn't take my calls. I told Dee I had had enough of Earlie as good as he was and enough of claiming. I wanted Wiggy Ramos and I wanted an allowance race. If Ten Taylor couldn't compete with the big boys for the big prizes I would consent to let him go in the smaller claimers and go on with my quest to find "the big horse." However, I was not prepared to let someone steal this prize before I could find out for myself. When Rejoie, a horse of equal value to Ten Taylor Road, was claimed for $25,000 the next day, I was more resolved to give the little black gelding just one more chance. I took the tag off his head and instructed Ernie to wait for the next available allowance race within my horse's conditions.

The phone rang early the next morning. It was Roger telling me that Ernie had told him that Ten Taylor had heat in his front right ankle and not to expect too many more races out of him. Roger insisted that this meant that we could not afford the luxury of an allowance race and that waiting for the end of July for non-winners of three would be foolish. As long as the horse was hurting I could not reject the idea of returning to the claiming ranks. I called Ernie and approved the 25,000 claiming race on July 19.

It was a sunny day but the track was listed as muddy. Ten Taylor loves the mud. We were running against the same horses that we had seen in the previous two races. Mission Highland and Cobar and two allowance horses that were dropping in class and one ambitious short claimer trying the big boys. As I stood in the paddock, I had a chance to jaw with Troy Patrick. I watched as he put the tongue tie on the horse and tightened the girth and exercised his knees. I asked Troy about the sore ankle. "What sore ankle?" was his response. "Every horse gets a little heat from time to time. There's nothing wrong with the horse." I've been had again by Ernie, I thought. The horse was running at the right level for the wrong reason. You can't win with Ernie. I refused to say anything before the race but I was contemplating capital punishment if my pony was taken.

The name of the game now is to win a race. Not just a stakes race or handicap or allowance, any race. Slowly but surely the reality that Ten Taylor Road would never become a "big horse" was becoming apparent.

When I arrived at the paddock that day, Dick and George Reynolds were there to greet me with "No question you're going to get claimed today…don't forget to keep the halter." I smiled at them knowing that the kidding was all in good fun. I quipped back at Dick, "Don't be surprised if someone leads away your number one money maker today," as I noted in the form that Dick had dropped his allowance horse to $16,000.

Dick is the kind of guy who likes to "run a horse at you." The term applies to owners and trainers who drop a horse into such a low level that one is immediately suspicious that the horse must be hurt. No one claims the horse and it usually keeps winning at that level while the world waits for it to fall apart. Most trainers will stay away from a horse that is dropping so severely.

This is where I met jockey Wiggy Wigberto Ramos for the first time. The man belongs in the Hall of Fame. He was instructed to take the horse to the lead and stay there.

Ten Taylor came out of the gate like a bullet went to the lead in :22.0 flat, proceeded to turn :45.00 half and in the final furlong lost a front right shoe. Normally a horse will stop dead after losing a shoe, like a runner in a sprint losing a track shoe. The mud must have sucked the shoe right off. Instead, Double T's hung in there for a close second. Another $3,100 in the till and no wins. At least in the last few races we had managed two seconds and a third.

Troy was happy with the race but still commented to me on the way back to the paddock "He ain't the horse he was last year." I had a feeling that we were stuck on this level for a while. I was ready to concede that another claimer was the solution when I heard over the loud speaker, "Claimed in the last race was Samurai Warrior." We had again dodged a bullet.

We were running on Murphy's Law. "Anything that can go wrong, will go wrong." Even though we had come out of the allowance ranks we still had not won a race. How could I argue against Roger and Ernie when another 6 1/2 furlong claim came up the beginning of August. I called in and found out that we would be running again against the same horses that were in the last race.

As a footnote to the last race, the only other horse claimed that day besides Samurai Warrior was Dick's horse. He had won the race easily, but Dick couldn't fool J.R. Smith Jr. who snapped up the colt for less than a quarter of what the horse had won the last year. I couldn't wait to see Dick to rub it in.

It did not take much convincing to run Ten Taylor back on August 1 at the same level and against the same competition. With Ramos on his back and everything that could happen already having happened, this was a sure thing.

Someone forgot to tell Cobar and Devil's Claw. After getting stuck in the gate, we came out again on top at the first call in :22 flat and ran a quick half at :44.4. Cobar caught us at six furlongs in 1:10 3/5 and went on to a five length victory at 1:16 2/5 for 6 1/2 furlongs. Devil's Claw caught us at the wire and we had another third place check for $1,700.

I visited Ten Taylor in his stall after the race. I fed him a couple of carrots. It was a quiet, cool and delightful afternoon. I looked into his glassy eyes, which seemed to only be focused on the carrots in my right hand and I conceded to myself that maybe this was not "the big horse." Maybe, Missy's filly or better yet, Out for a Spin, would make my dream come true. Right now, however, good horse sense dictated that we drop to a level where he could win. The condition book had a race for $18,000 on August 11. I called Ernie and left a message.

I am presumptive in assuming that most of you reading this have never experienced the frustration involved in attempting to match a horse with a race. It would seem so simple a task. Just find a race and enter a horse. The racing secretary at each track prepares, some two weeks in advance, a condition book which creates a tentative racing schedule containing from nine to fifteen races per day. The races are separated by the sex and age of the horse, the number of races the horse has won, the length of the race, and whether the horses running in the race are eligible to be claimed.

The job of the racing secretary is to anticipate the number of horses in each category on the grounds in order to make up fair and interesting races. When the track offers large stakes races or handicap races they invite, and welcome, outside entries. It is a rare occurrence to see a horse shipped in for a small claiming race.

Each time a six furlong race for three and up horses came up with a claiming tag of between $18,000 and $25,000, the secretary at Arlington could only find two or three horses willing to run. We had to settle for a seven furlong event on August 23. Ten Taylor was ready to run, and running him in a longer race was more acceptable than not running him at all.

A 4-year old colt by the name of Distinct Leader ran the seven furlongs in 1:23 flat. He passed up a tired Ten Taylor Road who led again at six furlongs at a fast 1:093/5. We picked up $780 for holding on to fourth. Where do we go now?

*"You do not have to see a race to find out if you won or lost, just wait until the next day and see how many people ask you to repay their losing tickets."*

CHAPTER **17**

# THE BEGINNING OR THE END

"Drop him to $10,000" was all that I heard the next day. This horse is insured for almost $100,000 and they want me to put a $10,000 tag on him? I truly want to convey my feelings at this point. I refuse to give in to the temptation to play the game the way everyone else does. I keep hearing the words of Dick "Don't hang on to a loser, Lee, they keep making horses every day." What he says makes sense, but I am just too damn stubborn.

I looked into the new condition book and saw another claiming race for $18,000 at six furlongs. If we get lucky enough for that race to fill, maybe we can stay at this level.

Ernie reluctantly entered Ten Taylor in the Labor Day event telling me that we were wasting our time.

The day of the race found Ernie in the paddock saddling the horse. He had fired Troy and was without an assistant trainer. Dee was about to visit her sister and Ernie was desperate to find a new assistant. I hoped that the new assistant would be a younger man with some new and progressive ideas.

Ernie told me he had changed the bit that Ten Taylor was running with to a softer one. At first this change seemed counterproductive. The horse had failed to keep a straight course in several races and even became disqualified once. The jockeys who have ridden him always have complained that he runs his own race and with a softer bit the jockey's ability to rate the horse would be limited.

The eight horse field was pretty impressive for a mid level claimer, boasting several horses that had passed the $250,000 mark in earnings. Ten Taylor Road came up as a 5-1 shot. Not all of his fans had left him yet including some of the newspapers who were giving predictions that he was "due to pop."

Labor Day 1993 turned out to be one of those summer days you live for. Mid-seventies, blue skies and not a cloud in sight. The wind was so calm that your words fell straight to the ground. I looked Ten Taylor Road right in the eye in the paddock and I told him "Buddy, it's now or never." The horse was unusually calm and was not frothing at the mouth or trying to play with the bit as usual. He paraded around the horseshoe shaped Arlington Park paddock with his head high. His black coat shone in the sun and the groom had braided his hair back for this race. I felt a special excitement as several of my racing friends waved at me from behind the fence.

If only he could win this race we might be able to go forward again. I was afraid to raise my hopes. My betting reflected my feelings as I only put $100 to win on him together with a $50 perfecta boxing him with a horse called Tumbleweed ridden by Mark Guidry.

As Double T's left the paddock area with Wiggy on

his back, I shouted to Ramo, "Numero uno," and raised up my index finger. Ramos responded with a little tip of his cap. I got to my seat the same minute the bell went off. Spencer, my son, had brought some girlfriends and people from our office to the track. Even he had trepidation in advising his crowd to bet on our horse. Together they must have had only $10 wagered.

Ten Taylor broke evenly but not on the lead. At the first call he was a comfortable third in an average :22 3/5. By comparison it was very slow for him and normally I would have expected him to be able to lead at that speed. Wiggy seemed to be rating the horse despite the soft bit.

Around the turn they came with Prince Compliance first, C.J's Lucky Boy second and Ten Taylor Road and Tumbleweed a modest distance back. I looked at the board, :46 seconds at the second call and :58 2/5 at the third. Was Ten Taylor Road losing it or was Wiggy the first jockey to be able to rate the horse? It was only going to take seconds to find out.

I couldn't help watching Guidry, the master of rating, changing leads on Tumbleweed and starting his charge. He came on as only Guidry could ride a horse off the pace. I watched as Tumbleweed, the number one horse, on the rail flew past the tiring leaders who had hooked up in a speed duel and all I could think of was another fourth.

I could not believe my eyes, Guidry was flying by the leaders on the rail and Ramos was flying by the leaders on the outside. The finish line, so help me, appeared to be moving toward the horses as fast as they approached it. Everything sped up as though time was multiplied by ten. I never really saw the finish. The slow motion replay revealed

Ramos pushing down hard on the head of Ten Taylor just at the wire and the width of a nose hair separating the two.

After a five minute wait, the photo sign stopped flashing and the win place and show sign lit up with a large white announcement 2-1-6. I looked back at Ten Taylor Road, displaying a large number two on his back heading for the winner's circle with Wiggy proudly holding his left index finger up waving at me shouting..."Numero uno." Fourteen months of waiting had finally produced a win.

I ran toward the winner's circle giving high-fives and saying my hellos to a multitude of well-wishers. Roger and I embraced, Spin and I shook hands and I turned to kiss Paula and remembered that she was at home preparing our annual Labor Day pool party and end of summer bash. I couldn't wait to get to a phone to call her. A small trophy was given to us in honor of "Fantastic Sam's" whatever the hell that is, and Roger and I ran to the cages to grab our loot. Surprising enough the horse paid $13 to win and $51 on the perfecta box with Tumbleweed. I kicked myself to think that I did not have enough confidence to bet more.

I called Ernie a few days after the race and told him that I had decided to run Ten Taylor Road in a five furlong turf race for a purse of $30,000 on the last day of the season at Arlington. The race was named "the Taylor Special" and seemed to me to be short enough for Double T's to compete in. Further, we had never tried him on the turf and it seemed a good time to experiment. Dee agreed with me but Ernie was resistant to the idea of Ten Taylor competing with such tough speed and told me that he didn't want me to kill the horse.

Roger was cool on the idea because it would mean over a month layoff and since his standardbreds ran every hour on the hour like the local bus, he didn't have the patience to wait a month between races. I made a concession with Ernie and Roger in that if a good allowance race came up in the last condition book at Arlington, I would consider changing my position. However, I told both of them that Ten Taylor had run his last claiming race and that his win should earn him a trip back to the big leagues.

The month of September swiftly disappeared without a six furlong allowance event meeting our horse's conditions. There was one last sprint at the end of the month which would subject Ten Taylor again to a claiming tag of $25,000.

Again came those little voices from the same mavens (experts) who tell you not to fall in love with a horse and to run the animal as low as it can go and as many times as it can go and then dump him and start over again. I have committed myself to the task of finding a "big horse" and the fact that Ten Taylor has, at this point in time, earned almost $100,000 for Roger and I, gives me the perseverance to stick it out with him.

Again the little voices won out and my proud gelding was put on the block for two bits in a six furlong test against a pretty impressive field. Everybody else was trying to win just one more for the Gipper before they moved on to Keeneland or to warmer climates. Many trainers, who might not want to carry marginal animals with them, put them on the block at the end of a season.

Instead of being a cakewalk, we were in some pretty tough company. Ramos was again selected to ride Ten Taylor Road. I decided that it was time for me to put more than just my checkbook into his racing career. I had been keeping videotapes of all of Ten Taylor's races, which were broadcast on a local station each morning, and reviewing the films.

I noticed that each time he was whipped in the left rear he lugged out to the right and when hit in the right he veered to the left. All of the jockeys we had employed to date beat the shit out of the horse coming out of the turn and down the stretch. Ten Taylor would lurch first left and then right as he tacked down the stretch, running an extra eighth of a furlong and chancing disqualification with each move.

I mentioned this fact to Bobby Baird and he told me that his trip to the Hall of Fame was financed by his ability to show the horse the whip and not have to use it all the time. I told this to Ernie who put me down with the comment, "What do you want me to do? Tell the jock to tickle him under the nose?" Ernie was unsuccessful in trying to make shit out of me, because I planned to make sure that Ramos got the message before the next race.

I still had not abandoned the idea of running in the five furlong turf event even though it was only 11 days after this race, especially since I still feared losing my horse in a claim.

Ernie put that idea to bed when he told me that he had entered The Ghost in that race because Dick had the same idea.

Right now I have had just about enough of running in the shadow of Dick's 3-year old. I didn't concede the point to Ernie but felt that I would let the results of the race speak for me.

The six furlong claiming race saw Ten Taylor going off as a surprising 5-1 shot. A horse named Glass Town, who, as a sprinter, had beaten almost everything in sight, had dropped to a claimer. The remaining field consisted of one horse who had given Ten Taylor a run for his money a few races back, named Samurai Warrior, and several other horses who had earned anywhere from $100,000 to $300,000 in their careers.

I caught Ramos before Ernie did and I told him, in no uncertain terms, that I did not want him to use the whip on Ten Taylor. He shook his head in an understanding nod and turned to Ernie who whispered something to him.

The gate opened and out shot Ten Taylor Road. The heavy favorite Glass Town attacked quickly. Ten Taylor hooked up in a speed battle with the challenger. Out of the turn they came, Ten Taylor Road and Glass Town and suddenly there was only Ten Taylor Road.

I could see him clearly as his lead built up. Wiggy Ramos, contrary to my desires, was beating the shit out of Ten Taylor, first left handed then right then left. The gelding tacked toward the finish line seemingly unopposed until caught at the wire in a photo finish by Samurai Warrior. You could fit no more that a sheet of paper between the noses of the two horses but it still meant a second place instead of a first for Ten Taylor Road and possibly a step in the wrong direction.

Everybody congratulated us at the big race he had run and there was a lot of back slapping and ticket waving which went unnoticed by me until I saw our groom safely leading away my horse unclaimed. I caught sight of Ernie and yelled, "No mas baby!" Which meant an end to the claimers.

The loss convinced Ernie that the horse did not belong in such a tough field of speed horses as would be entered in the five furlong turf event. He promised me that if I gave up the idea of running, he would be able to get a race the first week of Hawthorne at an allowance level for six furlongs. I conferred with Roger and since both of us were going out of town that week we agreed to let Ernie wait until Hawthorne opened up.

I visited Ten Taylor in his stall after the narrow loss to Samurai Warrior and the first thing I noticed were the large white patches of salve on his flank covering the welts and wounds caused by the beating he had received coming down to the wire. I promised the horse that no one else would ever hit him like that again. I made peace with him by an offering of carrots and nose scratches and left the barn resolved to take charge of the situation.

Ernie ran The Ghost in the turf event and the horse set a new track record of :57 flat beating the field by almost two lengths. That certainly established him as a power in the sprinting ranks and left us still a question mark. One thing was not in doubt. No matter how much anyone else told me to run the horse down in claimers, Ten Taylor Road was not for sale. I am in search of "the big horse," and until proven otherwise, I will put all my faith in this little black diamond.

*"My wife said it quite clearly:.'What do you expect from that horse, he's only human.'"*

CHAPTER **18**

# THE DREAM RETURNS

Ernie had found a new assistant trainer, a young man by the name of Pat Devereaux. Pat had been with a trainer named Granitz prior to this time and looked like a real find. He was able to relieve Ernie of a lot of the back breaking work that was plaguing him, and I could tell that the marriage was a good one. I tried to talk to Pat about Ten Taylor and my observations but he was smart enough to follow Ernie's admonition and keep his mouth shut to owners. The worst thing an assistant trainer can do is try to talk to owners. This is like a lawyer's secretary giving legal advise over the phone to clients. You never know when you are going to contradict something your boss said and cause friction.

Ten Taylor Road looked to be at the top of his game as Paula and I left for my niece's wedding in Cabo San Lucas. Ernie promised me a race the first Monday that Hawthorne opened up but when I called from Mexico I found out that we were not in the race and I was furious. "Ernie!" I yelled long distance, "if that fucking horse doesn't run this week I'm going to change barns!" I slammed the phone down and told Paula that if this horse had to sit and wait for a race for the next two weeks I was going to make some calls and switch trainers.

At this point it is imperative that I explain that I have come to understand there is a serious love-hate relationship between owners and trainers. It is the same relationship owners of baseball or football teams have with their managers. The manager or trainer is clearly the expert and has the experience and the knowledge necessary to run the club or train the horse and all the owner has is the ball. When the owner feels like it, he takes the ball and goes home and the game is over. The trainer or manager therefore, must find a way to both do his job and keep the ball.

I like Ernie. In fact, I respect him and look up to him. But at the same time, I don't trust him or any other trainer, and I wouldn't be surprised to find out that he likes me and still thinks that I am a schmuck with a checkbook. Notwithstanding all of the above, I was not about to watch and let a horse at the top of his game sit idle. I was prepared to raise hell with Ernie the first thing Tuesday morning when I got home.

When I returned to Northbrook late Monday night, I was able to reach Bloodstock Research on my computer and check the races for Wednesday at Hawthorne. That is to say I was able to do so in between running to the bathroom to answer the call of a newly-acquired case of "Montezuma's Revenge" that I had imported from Mexico. I was shocked to find that Ten Taylor was entered in the seventh race Wednesday against a field of some of the fastest horses left in the Chicago area, including a horse named Stalwars.

Let me tell you about Stalwars. When I was growing up, my hero in baseball was Ernie Banks. My football idol was Gayle Sayers and in the last five years of horse racing I never missed a bet on Stalwars. This 8-year old horse, by Stalwart, had earned just over $1,150,000 and even at his advanced age had won four out of nine this year for almost $300,000. He had just come out of races such as the Fort Dearborn Handicap, Iselin Handicap, The Washington Park, Cicero Mile and had been the winner of the Budweiser Breeders' Cup at six furlong, qualifying him to be known as one of the fastest horses in America. Just 90 days ago he had run fourth to Valley Crossing, Devil his Due and Bertrando, top contenders for horse of the year.

What in the hell were we doing running against this class of horse? The other horses in the race read like a who's who of speed in Illinois and the race was just an allowance for $21,600.

We were made an entry with Marlene and Earl Silver's Tory Sound, who had set the track record for six furlongs last year and even though not at the top of his game, was by no means a pushover. I almost felt Ernie was punishing me for pushing him into finding a race. To add insult to injury, Ernie had hired Randy Meier to ride Ten Taylor Road knowing that I was still angry at that last ride he gave Our Tsunami Su.

Randy had been the leading jockey at Hawthorne last year, but had fallen in my disfavor when he buried Our Tsunami Su on the rail in the mud and Ernie knew that he was the last jock I wanted on my horse. I knew Randy's agent Tom Morgan, who was a friend of John Hildebrand and sat near us at Arlington. Tom was a good sort and as a favor to him and the Hildebrands, I didn't make a stink.

When I reached Ernie to ask him about the race all

he could say was "Looks like you are in pretty tough." Was that an understatement! The thing I could not get through my head was that Ernie was pushing me to drop the horse down with claimers saying that he didn't want the horse to get beat up. He didn't want Ten Taylor to run against The Ghost and Bonita Devil on the sod at five furlongs but he had put us in against Stalwars? This was, to me, like saying I don't want you to play college football, it's too rough...go play with the Chicago Bears.

On the other hand this was Ten Taylor's chance to prove to himself, me and the rest of the Chicago racing world that he was ready to make himself a factor in the local scene again. A respectable showing here would earn him the right to go in handicap and stakes races again. A win would be more than I could expect. This was the time that the coach sends in the rookie quarterback, hands him the ball and says "Let's see what you got."

Hawthorne Race Course was like a ghost town. In comparison to the thousands of race fans that flock to the serene grass and flower covered paddock areas of Arlington, Hawthorne offered only a cement patio surrounded by the slums of Chicago. I was dressed in a sport coat that I had worn to the office and stuck out in the crowd of racetrack junkies like a pen in a pencil box. I found Ernie sprawled across a couch just inside the paddock area sneezing and wiping the feverish sweat of a 2-day old cold off his brow.

He looked up at me and said, "You just missed it, I had a $38 winner...da two horse of Dick's." Translated, he had told me that Dick 's new 2-year old filly had won and paid almost $40 for a $2 win ticket.

"How are we going to run?" I asked. "Horse is at

the top of his game...gonna run big," was his response.

Just then Marlene Silver and Dee Poulos entered the paddock area. We shared greetings and Marlene and I wished each other well. We had talked about someday running as an entry and here we were. I truly hoped that if we had to get beat it would be by her horse, Tory Sound. Marlene had little hopes, however, for that happening. She and her partner had been quite disappointed at how the horse had been running of late and had no realistic expectations of winning.

We made our bets and I headed for the paddock to meet the jockey. I beat Ernie to Randy Meier. I greeted Meier with a handshake and told him that I was glad to see him on my horses again. I told him in no uncertain terms not to hit my horse and only show him the whip. He nodded at me the same way Ramos, Guidry, Baird, Seville and the rest of the other jockeys did and headed to talk to Ernie.

Ernie, a giant of a man, towered over the jock as he gave instructions and the scene always looked like Jonah and the Whale. I could almost imagine that he was saying, "Don't listen to that Jagoff, just do what I say." However, I don't know for sure what his instructions were. Ernie turned quickly to Earlie Fires who was riding Tory Sound and whispered something else. As fast as I can describe it, they were heading for the starting gate.

I chose to watch the race from inside the glass on the TV even though it was a beautiful 65 degree day. Hawthorne does not have a large screen television in the centerfield to watch the race on, and from the rail it is difficult to pick up the horses as they come out of the turn.

The bell sounded and Ten Taylor Road sprang from

the gate together with Mission Highland like two shells shot out of a cannon. The two were joined quickly by the other speed in the race as the favorite, Stalwars sat off the pace last. The quarter went in :22 2/5 and found Ten Taylor Road in the lead by a length. I glanced at the times for most other horses that day and found that the track was unusually slow and that most horses were turning :24 and :25 for the first call. Could Ten Taylor sustain such speed against such powerful closers as Position of Power and Stalwars?

Coming out of the turn all you could hear was Kurt Becker, the announcer, shouting "and here comes Stalwars...fifth, fourth, third...he is charging at the leader Ten Taylor Road."

I watched as Randy continued to hand ride my horse. Until now he had not touched the animal and now, when he needs to make the horse move to hold off the stampeding Stalwars, how would he do it? I leaned closer to the TV screen and watched as Meier showed the whip to Double T's. He never hit him! He waved the whip along side of his nose as if to remind the horse that he could use it. Ten Taylor responded as he had almost a year before. He reached down into his big heart and answered Meier with a charge that met the challenge of Stalwars. All I could hear was Kurt Becker's voice yelling, "It's not enough...it's not enough...Stalwars can't catch Ten Taylor Road...he is going to taste defeat." With that I watched Ten Taylor Road cross the finish line a good length and a quarter ahead of Stalwars.

I jumped over the chairs and tried to find an exit to the winners circle. I hugged Dee and Marlene, shook Ernie's hand and yelled my congratulations to Randy. All was forgiven.

We lined up for a photo, but Ernie left the line and picked up the telephone to the stewards. He held up his forefinger as if to say wait a minute. He shouted over to me, "They're gonna take your number down for a foul." I glanced over my shoulder at the tote board which already read "OFFICIAL" and I gave Ernie the finger. As sick as he was and as pissed off at me as he was and as wrong as he was, he had to have the last laugh and the last word.

Even as he saw that the joke was over he continued to talk to a "ghost steward" on a dead phone line, pretending to be arguing our case against disqualification. I lined up for the photo and smiled at Ernie and after the photo I gave him a wink. It truly is a love-hate relationship.

As Meier dismounted and returned from the weigh-in I shook his hand once more and said, "Looks like I found a rider...the mount is yours." He thanked me for the ride, and all the feelings that I had harbored against him for the last year drained from me.

I gave Ten Taylor a kiss on the nose as the groom led him away and for the first time in seven races I did not have to wait until after the time for the claiming announcements.

Although not a particularly fast time, until another horse betters it, the time set by Ten Taylor Road this day will appear each day in the Hawthorne program and will read..."FASTEST TIME 1993...TEN TAYLOR ROAD, 1:10 2/5, 10/13/93." My dream was alive.

I couldn't wait until his next race. The new condition book for Hawthorne listed the same allowance conditions for October 23rd. Ernie was always reluctant to send a class animal right back into a race unless he was absolutely certain that the horse would not be hurt by the short rest. There are several horses Ernie calls "weekend warriors" that run whenever and wherever they can qualify for a race. For the "weekend warrior" every race might be their last, and the owner and trainer are trying to squeeze every last nickel out of the horse before the inevitable happens.

The next few days found Ernie laying a trip on me again about how Double T's was not eating well and that we should skip the 23rd. Somehow I smelled "The Ghost" lurking in the shadows. If the race came up easy this would be like stealing $12,500 for Dick and his new partners. Ernie kept telling me that he didn't want to beat the horse up and that we had something good going now. It seemed strange to me that just two short races ago the horse was supposedly picking up heat in his ankle and looked like we should drop him like a sack of potatoes. Now all of a sudden we are protecting this gem again.

Two days before the race, Ernie called and told me he thought the horse was eating good again and that we could run him on the 23rd. I called Roger to tell him the good news. Roger told me he had found out that Dick was intending to run The Ghost in that race but when he found out that Stalwars would be running again that he and Ernie decided they didn't want to hurt The Ghost by running against such stiff competition. Besides, the name of the game is making money and it made no sense to Dick to place a horse in a race he could not win.

However, in we went. It made some sense to me. We had just beaten Stalwars and had come out of the race capable of running again in 10 days.

The experts all had the race picked the same way. Even though we had beaten "the big horse" just a few days ago, everyone was picking Stalwars over us and leaving the rest of the field out of the race. Stalwars was a morning line favorite at 6-5 and we were 8-5. The remainder of the field was made up of the same horses as the race before with the addition of two horses that stood no chance whatsoever.

Roger ran into Dick at Trackside OTB just before the race. Dick told Roger that I was pretty stupid putting my horse in a race where he could not compete and that this field would blow us away. He told Roger to bet on us to "live." Dick said Stalwars would put us away by 10 lengths and our horse wouldn't run for another three months after being exhausted by the run. Roger was so taken aback that he didn't even bet our race.

October 23,1993, would be a pretty big day for me, running against a "big horse" and celebrating my wife's 50th birthday with a surprise party that night. I asked customer service at Hawthorne to name a race in honor of Paula and they complied by naming the 12th race that day "The Paula Forman 50th Birthday Race." Two years ago I had to pay to get into the races and now the track would recognize my request, such as naming a race after my wife, by making a simple phone call. We had come a long way.

We assumed our customary positions at the trackside after making our bets, and after five furlongs, the race set up the same exact way as the first event. There were only two major differences from the first. Ten Taylor had earned a high weight of 122 pounds, up five pounds, while Stalwars gained only two pounds to 119. We were now spotting the big horse three pounds. That's comparable to me spotting Arnold Palmer three strokes. What A Romeo, a horse that usually comes from off the pace, decided to hook up with

Ten Taylor in a speed duel and did not allow us to get a relaxed and uncontested lead. These two factors allowed Stalwars to catch Ten Taylor at the wire for a length victory while the rest of the field rambled in one at a time well behind.

I looked up at the fractions. The first quarter split of :22 2/5 was good. The :44 4/5 at the half was spectacular. However, the time of our lead we had on Stalwars at five furlongs was clocked at :56 3/5 which was a fifth of a second faster than any horse had run five furlongs at Hawthorne in the last three years. The race was run in 1:09 1/5 which meant Ten Taylor Road had run faster than he had ever run in his career.

I noticed several of Ten Taylor's fans applauding him as he left the infield, even though he had lost. I joined in the applause. There was little shame in splitting decisions with one of the best old-timers in the business. I felt a strange sense of accomplishment and a chill of excitement after the race.

Granted, we had lost and the $4,200 check for second place that followed was a far cry from the $12,600 the owners of Stalwars picked up that day, but we had competed with some of the best and walked away healthy and with our heads high. Just as important, I had been exonerated in my stubbornness not to give up on Ten Taylor and not to allow him to be claimed or run with the other dog meat that make up the other eight races after the feature events. I couldn't wait to see Dick and ask him how he thought we had run. I figured I would tell Dick he was smart not to let his little pony run with competition like Stalwars and Ten Taylor Road.

Ernie was now talking about shipping the horse across the country and looking for major races. I remembered my goal, "to win a major stakes race" and to accomplish the ownership of a "big horse" and I thrilled in the thought that maybe, just maybe, Ten Taylor Road was it. Could I beat the odds? Could I win the lotto? Could I be the Walter Mitty who steps out of the mundane existence of a white-collar job to pitch a major league team to a World Series Victory? Would it be possible to hit the center of the target with the second horse you owned?

Stranger things have happened. Telly Sevalas, the actor, is a prime example. Telly had never owned a horse in his life when he dropped by producer Howard Koch's home. A local trainer by the name of Mel Stute was trying to talk Koch into buying a horse for $6,000 and Sevalas, on a whim, bought the horse in partnership with Koch and named it Telly's Pop in honor of the candy he was using to give up his smoking habit.

Telly's Pop won several hundreds of thousands of dollars and was one of California's top 3-year olds when he broke down. Sevalas never bought another horse. I played poker with Telly at the Dunes hotel in Las Vegas that year and although when I met him I had not yet given birth to the idea of writing this book, I now look back at him as an example of the possibilities for success that this game holds.

As I set these thoughts to paper now, I remember the words of a fortune teller I had hired to entertain at my wife's surprise party, "Something that you have waited to finish for several years now will be successfully completed." she said. Could she have meant Ten Taylor Road?

*"A horserace differs from a beauty contest
in only one respect:
In a beauty contest the contestant whose nose goes over
the line first usually loses."*

CHAPTER **19**

# IN SEARCH OF
# THE BIG RACE

We were now again faced with the problem of finding races for Ten Taylor Road. When you have a claimer who can go long and short, the books are full of suitable races. When you have a sprinter eligible for allowance, handicap and stakes races, you have to look far and wide. Sportsman's Park, where Ten Taylor had great success as a 3-year old, would not open until early February. We could look forward to the Johnston Memorial and Budweiser Breeders' Cup in March and the Cicero Mile in April.

Earl Silver suggested we look at Remington Park in Oklahoma where they run some $50,000 sprint handicaps. I personally would prefer having the horse down in Florida where I could watch him run over Christmas vacation. When I approached Ernie with the idea of moving the horse to a warmer climate he was not too receptive. I kept remembering Ernie telling Roger and me that during 1993 we would be traveling quite a bit with this horse looking for the big races. To date, our longest trip has been from Arlington

Park to Hawthorne, a distance of 20 miles over the world's fastest freeway.

I feel that Ernie and I have grown apart. Our method of doing business with each other consists of my calling Dee to inform her of an idea to convey to Ernie, and Ernie calling Roger to talk me out of my idea. I called Dee to tell her I wanted Ernie to have a game plan for our horse now that it was running at the top of its game.

Roger and I agreed that the most important item on our agenda for the horse would be a game plan for the next three months or until Sportsman's Park opened up. We both agreed that the horse should be given an opportunity to run with the "big horses" to establish himself, and that since Hawthorne Park did not offer this opportunity to sprinters, we should look elsewhere or rest the horse for Sportsman's Park.

Ernie called me immediately after I had spoken to Roger. Before I could get a word in, he began to expound as to how I was going to run Ten Taylor into the ground by racing him too often and that he refused to enter him this Sunday. This caught me by surprise as I had not contemplated running the horse until the first week in November. I hardly said a word as Ernie went on and on listing the virtues of properly resting the animal.

Friday afternoons usually find both Roger and I at Trackside OTB. I walked in and sat down beside Roger who was suffering from the world's worst cold. He looked at me with a childish grin and said, "We are in Sunday." I gave him a smile, and extended the middle finger on my right hand while closing the remaining fingers in a fist and went right on with my handicapping. "We are in Sunday," he repeated again without moving a muscle and then went on to tell me that Ernie had entered Ten Taylor Road in an allowance race for this Sunday. This was less than 24 hours after beating on me about giving the horse a rest. Even more unbelievable was the fact that we were the number eight horse in the eighth race, my luckiest post position. This was great, but what happened to Ernie's game plan? I thought I was the fucking idiot who wanted to run the horse back so quickly.

I called Ernie who responded by telling me that the horse was kicking the stall down and his blood came back perfect and, in this condition, he could run all night and day.

I pulled up the race on my computer and was instantly shocked to see he was in a field of 10 of the very best horses left at Hawthorne. Even without Stalwars, the list read like an all-star team of sprinters. Every horse in the field had earned over $100,000 lifetime and each had earned the right to be considered the favorite. My computer had Ten Taylor Road an even money favorite with Mission Highland and Glass Town second and third at 5-1. The race was at a scheduled six furlongs with a purse of $21,000. The field would have justified a $50,000 purse. The track had purchased an event cheaply enough. The contestants were eagerly awaiting the challenge of being victorious in such a prestigious field.

We again went through the same rituals which led us up to race time with the exception that I had made a selection for the twin trifecta races that preceded our race that day, which found me with eight winning exchange tickets for a pot of over $170,000. I ordinarily do not want to bet on the race before ours as I want to concentrate on our race. This day found me in a rush trying to handicap the seventh race to search for the right combination to a pot of gold.

I quickly turned to Forman's rule of handicapping. After circling the best Beyer times on the sheet and noting the best speed ratings and earnings for the horses in the race I turned to my parking ticket which contained the number 832 and boxed 8, 3 and 2 for six of my tickets and 8 in front of 2 and 1 for the other two.

As an indication of what kind of a day this would be, the seventh race found the number 1 horse, Vanna D, winning the race at 9-1 and the favored 8 horse coming in third behind the 2 . The winning combination was 1, 2 and 8 in that order. If I had arrived at the parking lot twenty cars earlier I would have left with exactly $178,600.

With my heart still pounding from the excitement of the seventh race, I watched as Ten Taylor was loaded into the starting gate. I noticed his head flail to the right and the gate assistant starter grab his harness and yank his head violently to the left and slam it into the side of the starting gate just as the bell went off and the gate opened. I was expecting Double T's to bolt to the lead as usual and was dumbfounded to see him fail to leave the gate. Ten Taylor was dead last at the start, a good solid 15 lengths off the pace when he was expected to be on the lead.

Jockey Randle Meier made a bold attempt to return the horse to the field but at the first call the best he could do to catch this type of speed was to be ninth. These horses were not puppy chow and the leaders, Mission Highland and Glass Town, turned fractions of :22 and :44 flat. As the field turned for home I could see Ten Taylor Road among the leaders. I looked away in disgust expecting him to finish nearly dead last when I heard the track announcer giving him a call saying something about how well Ten Taylor was coming on at the leaders. As the horses crossed the finish line I was astounded to see Ten Taylor Road, who had gone to the rail and worked his way up to the leaders, involved in a photo finish for second place.

He lost the photo. However, the horse had proven to me, the crowd and to the rest of the racing public that even in losing he was a superior animal. Ten Taylor Road had been able to make up all but 3 lengths of the 10 or so he had spotted the leaders and had closed on a field whose winner had run in 1:09.

We had again been the victim of racing luck. I am certainly better capable now of understanding what this means. In each sport there is an element of skill and an element of luck. The way the ball bounces on any given play can change the outcome in any baseball, football or basketball game. In horseracing you have to be both good and lucky at the same time. Today we were just good.

Seven days later I found myself glued to the television screens circling our local OTB as the high holiday of horseracing was being celebrated this year at Santa Anita Park. The Breeders' Cup and its seven sacred races were being televised around the world. Unfortunately, I was still on the outside looking in. A mere spectator. I felt like Tiny Tim on Christmas, peering through the butchers window at the prize goose hanging in the shop waiting for the rich kid to come along and take it home to dinner.

Seven owners would share the Oscar of racing today, the beautiful Breeders' Cup. Seven horses would walk away with the title "big horse" and one would be crowned Horse of the Year. I tried to put myself in their shoes and contemplate for a brief moment what each of the owners and trainers must feel like today.

I am now looking for a "big race" for Ten Taylor Road and then along comes the Breeders' Cup and diminishes the importance of any allowance or handicap race I could contemplate as being big. However, in skimming through the program I came to the last race, the Classic, with a prize of $3,000,000. The winner can almost be assured a majority vote in Horse of the Year balloting. Who was the favorite this year? Bertrando, the horse that had just beaten Stalwars, while losing to Valley Crossing, in the Iselin Handicap in July. The same Stalwars who had been beaten by none other than Ten Taylor Road.

Again, in looking at the sprint, a six furlong event for $1,000,000 I kept coming across a contestant who was constantly in the money in all of the big sprint races across the United States...none other than Black Jack Road, another sprinter by Kennedy Road. Suddenly, I felt just a little bit closer to my goals like the door had been opened a tiny bit and although not invited to the party, I had been able to sneak into the kitchen to watch through the crack in the door.

As each race ended and each victor was awarded his cup, my heart grew more and more lustful for such a prize. However, as in the case of the pauper who watches the prince being crowned, I knew in my heart it may never be. These winners were, by in large, the product of millions of dollars spent on breeding and lifetimes of attempts at grabbing the golden ring. How could I, with only two years of experience, and a horse purchased for a $20,000 tag have the audacity to yearn for such a prize?

I returned to reality the next evening when I called Ernie about 5 p.m. to ask him if a game plan had been established. You would think that I had set off a bomb in his house the way he tore into me for waking him up. How in the hell did I know that he goes to bed before 6 p.m.? In between apologies, I heard Ernie say that he had asked the people at Hawthorne to put up another race like the one we had just lost for this weekend and they agreed to do so. This would give us a shot at a nice purse just before the Thanksgiving Classic for $25,000. Neither of the races would be considered major, however it did give Roger and I a chance to pick up more than $27,000 in prize money in less than two weeks. If we could win both of the races we felt both the horse and our pocketbooks would survive our search for a big race for a while.

I can't blame Ernie, but the six furlong event before Thanksgiving never materialized. Every time the race was put up, not enough horses were around to run. Everyone seemed to be waiting for the Thanksgiving Day race. At this point I was beginning to wonder if we had not made a big mistake by not sending the horse out to Remington Park in Oklahoma where they were offering two six furlong events, each for $50,000.

I finally conceded to myself that giving the horse a month off and waiting for the handicap race was a smart move. Every one of the top sprinters in the area would be in the event and it would be a great test for Ten Taylor.

I was comfortably watching the Saturday card from Hawthorne at Trackside when I was approached by Dick. After exchanging amenities I was promptly assaulted with the information that The Ghost would be entered in the

Thanksgiving Day sprint and that Dick didn't want the two speedsters in the same race again because they might hook up and allow a closer to steal the race. This was the same old tune with a different verse.

I was not about to let a month pass without a race and then take a pass on a $25,000 purse just so that The Ghost could run. Dick and I went nose to nose and he left threatening to tell Ernie that he had to choose between us and one of us would leave the barn. I told Dick to cool off and that I was certain we could work things out.

The Ghost had been sent to Churchill Downs and had not competed successfully there. Dick brought him back to Chicago and was trying to decide whether to send him to Florida for the winter or let him rest up here for the Sportsman's meeting.

I don't know if or how Ernie appeased Dick but we got the race and The Ghost was not in it. However, 11 of the best were, including Mission Highland and Glass Town.

My heart skipped a beat when I saw the headline in the Daily Racing Form the day of the Handicap. "Ten Taylor On Road to Success Again." He was again catching the eye of the public. He had beaten Stalwars, and had been trading punches with the best of the sprinters and now was slowly rising again, in the eyes of the experts, to the top of his game. I was very proud.

Thanksgiving Day came and Murphy's law came with it. Once again, we were interfered with at the start. Glass Town lunged out of the gate from post number 5 and quartered Ten Taylor Road who came out of the 6 hole. Ten Taylor was cut on the shin and fell back for an instant. He regained his stride and then took the lead at the first call. He led all the way around the track only to be caught at the wire by both Glass Town and Mission Highland. A third place finish and another excuse. There was no joy in Mudville. We were going sideways in our search for the big race.

I looked back at his record for 1993. We had run 16 times since April, which was quite a work load for any 4-year old, and we had won twice and had been second and third four times each. More importantly, he had cashed in each of his last 13 races and had made a profit for the year. The horse was healthy and still at the top of his game. If he quit today, he would have had, by any man's standards, an illustrious career. Whether he could become a "big horse" capable of winning "the big race" was the question still unanswered. One thing for sure, though, is that we had not quit and we were still in the hunt.

I have learned a lesson which is very important for me to pass on. It is the search for the prize that is the prize and the treasure itself. For when the hunt is over, only a memory remains. While the hunt is on however, the anticipation, the planning and the uncertainty are what makes life and the game more interesting.

In my quest for "the big horse" I have learned that in each of us may exist, dormant, a "big horse." We may never have the opportunity to win or even run the big race. However, winning the big race may not, in the long run, be the most valuable prize. The quest itself may be more valuable. He who reaches for the stars and fails may, in fact, have succeeded in gaining something more valuable than winning itself. A man's reach must exceed his grasp, or what is a heaven for. Man is limited not by his ability, but by the goals he sets. It is possible to reach out and touch a star.

My dad always told me the story of psychologists who placed twins into separate rooms for 24 hours. One room was full of toys and games and the other was three feet deep in horse manure. When the first room was opened, the one twin was sitting on a toy rocker, yawning and bored. He had played with everything in the room and nothing interested him anymore. When the second room was opened, the other twin was busy digging holes in the dung and was, at the time, engaged in tossing the manure in every direction. He had a big smile on his face as he whistled a happy tune and dispersed the horseshit. When asked by the psychologists what he was doing he replied…"with all this manure, there must be a pony in here somewhere."

I think I may be in room two.

*"Please let me break even today God, I need the money."*

CHAPTER **20**

## CROSSROADS

We came right back with a race against the same cast of characters including The Ghost. For an instant I had the urge to call Dick and ask him if he wanted to make a wager between our two horses. However, since his last comment I had mellowed and I was just interested in getting Ten Taylor back on top of his game.

It seems like he just isn't the same horse after getting stuck in the gate. He used to sprint out of the gate like a kid coming out of school at recess. Now, it seems as though he sloshes around in the gate when it opens like a Chevy with cheap tires in an ice storm.

This race was to be no different. Double T's came out of the gate sixth as The Ghost set a blistering first quarter. Ten Taylor caught the leaders in the stretch but the quick start had set the race up for the closers. The Ghost, Ten Taylor and Solar Gazor were caught at the wire and only Solar Gazor was able to hold on. It doesn't matter whether we lost by inches, feet or yards we still came in fifth while The Ghost was third.

Now all we had to look forward to was a long cold winter and seven weeks of no racing in Chicago. I told Ernie I wanted to send Ten Taylor Road somewhere warm for the winter and run in Louisiana or Florida. Ernie said Gulfstream in Miami was too tough a track and that all the New York horses go there for winter. They have a star system which makes it practically impossible to get a race unless you are a very high weight. At the same time, there was a horrendous fire at the Fair Grounds in Louisiana and their program was in jeopardy.

Ernie suggested Turfway Park in Kentucky. Turfway is just 10 miles south of Cincinnati in Florence, KY. Ernie had a friend, Peter Salmon, who was the head of the Kentucky Horsemen's, Benevolent and Protective Association and had the kind of savvy to get our horse into the right kind of stakes race. There were two six furlong races, each for $60,000, that looked good. With a little bit of luck, we could pay for the winter and come back to Sportsman's ready to run.

Kentucky has a way of discouraging outsiders from racing there. In each race we selected, the purse was $40,000 plus a $20,000 bonus for Kentucky bred horses only. In other words, outsiders are penalized quite a bit of the purse.

The first race was canceled because of 10 below zero weather in Kentucky. This type of weather was unheard of. The second race was canceled because of a snow storm which dumped 17 inches of snow on Lexington. Most of the horses were shippers and since highway 75 was closed, they closed the track.

We were able to catch a small allowance race at the end of January. Without a workout on the track and because Turfway had a night program, Ten Taylor was lost. Running on a strange track with a different jockey, and at night in the slop, he never picked up the track. It is like driving at night on a strange road in a snow storm, you may never exceed the speed limit and get passed up by locals who know every turn in the road.

Ten Taylor failed to cash and Ernie put him back on the first van to Chicago to prepare for opening day, February 14, at Sportsman's.

Ernie prepared Ten Taylor by working him out, first a short three furlong hop, and then five and six furlong jogs. Double T's responded with the three best works of the day in each event. If we could get the rest of the horses to run against us in the morning or if they paid for workouts, we could get rich.

I wanted to run in the opening day Valentine's Day Purse for $40,000. I knew every big sprinter at the track would be running for that kind of opening day money. Ernie felt the works, together with his condition, gave Ten Taylor a reasonable chance at the purse.

We had been blasted by heavy snow storms and below zero weather for most of the winter and the unusually mild and sunshiny weather of February 14 was a welcome relief. This was to be the day we would prove ourselves worthy of running with the likes of Stalwars, Jan Arctic, Big Twister and Position of Power. The track was listed as good, the sun was out and the weather was dry. We had pulled the rail and the number one post. Everything was set for our big attempt at an upset.

All the inside horses were winning in the opening races as the melting snow created a river in the middle of the track, leaving the rail dry. During the fifth race there was a spill and the stewards canceled the remainder of the card including our race. I sat for a good half hour after the stewards closed racing for the day and tried to figure out what happened to the $24,000 winner's share that I had already mentally spent.

Two weeks later we found an allowance race for non-winners of four other than maiden or claiming for a purse of $26.300. Tom Morgan, Randy Meier's agent, asked Ernie for another trip on the horse. Since Meier was the leading jock at Sportsman's, I felt he thought we had a shot at winning the allowance.

Coming out of the gate, Ten Taylor got bounced around pretty good by a 4-year old colt named Simply Outstanding. He never recovered and came in fifth. The stewards took Simply Outstanding down and placed us fourth. I walked away with a $1,600 slice of the purse and my tail between my legs. It seems that there is an excuse for every conceivable way of losing. When will racing luck turn in my favor again?

With the local Breeders' Cup $100,000 handicap coming up in only a month, I thought a tightener might be in order, followed by a two-week rest. Ernie nominated us and we had waited patiently through an exceptionally cold and snowy winter for the spring event. This race is one of many as a prelude to the $10 million dollar classic day in October. However, by this time, the thought of ever having an entry in the Classic, was a distant dream. In fact, Paula and I had made plans for a 30th anniversary cruise to Greece with Diane and Dr. Steve Labkon in October.

Not only had my bubble burst as to Ten Taylor Road becoming a "big horse" but my dreams of breeding a champion moved a step farther out of reach when Missy's Shystar was unable to top :28 flat handily for a quarter in two maiden tries at breezing as she clumsily waddled around the rail at Sportsman's exhibiting less talent for racing than my now 21-year old cat Frisky. Missy was destined to end up as a gentle saddle horse for Paula and Julie DePinto.

They say bad news comes in threes. Tim Kortgen, my trainer at Horizon Farms, gave me an update on my Media Starguest filly, Out for A Spin. It appears the filly, now a 2-year old, is parrot-mouthed, weak-hocked and has a belly full of worms. I almost fell out of my car when I drove up to the snow-filled paddock which held this under-sized, pot-bellied sow of a horse, who looked like a shaggy bear in hibernation. This was the progeny of the great Media Starguest? This was the flag bearer of my breeding dreams? Tim suggested that we not waste any more precious money on training and turn her out until summer to see if her hocks strengthen.

At this point in time, mid-March of 1994, my only wage earner has not won a race since October and has not exceeded a speed rating of over 78 in four races, I have lost my only filly with a knee problem, buried my gelding, and gifted my 3-year old as a saddle horse while finding out that my baby is a parrot-mouthed, pot-belly loser. And all this fun is costing me over $2,500 per month. I wondered if everyone in the business experiences these type of roller-coaster emotions.

A normal human being would call it a day, but not this dickhead. I have just agreed with Julie DePinto to bring back Moonlight Drive from New York. Julie's sister decided to quit the horse business in the east and move out west to become a productive member of society again. I agreed with Jeff and Peggy Matson to breed Moonlight to their Stallion,

Valid Appeal, if the Matsons would keep the mare for under $10 a day. With Roger sharing the risk this would only increase the insanity to another $150 a month.

The racing secretary at Sportsman's never brought the Valentines Day $40,000 race back but substituted a non-winners of four allowance for $26,300. Most of the big horses had run at a mile, and left some of the younger speed horses together with us in a small field of six for the race. This race left us with three weeks to rest before the Breeders' Cup and provided the tightener we needed. Randy Meier agreed to ride, which Roger and I allowed even though we felt that Randy kept coming up with encounters right out of the gate which may or may not have been a result of his own abilities. However, the fact that he was leading jockey at the meet led us to give him another chance. Just before the race, both Meier and his agent Morgan came down with the flu and C.H. Marquez Jr., who had ridden Tory Sound to a track record, agreed to take the ride.

One of the younger horses in the race, Pro Prospect had won its last three allowance races as it ran out its conditions. His last victory had been only two fifths of a second off the track record and a half second better than Ten Taylor's best effort at the top of his game. The other contestants had either won one of their last two races or had speed ratings in the 90s. I didn't think that even the Breeders' Cup would turn up so tough.

I will not glorify our third place finish, five lengths behind a 1:11 final time. However, Ten Taylor seemed to wake up as he earned a 73 speed figure with a rally from the rail. Marquees told me after the race he had tried to rate the horse and got stuck behind a slow horse as he made his move. He truly felt he could win with another chance on the horse.

Ernie and Pat had told me that Ten Taylor needed an easier race to gain back his confidence and this certainly was not it. His next endeavor would be a major stakes race for $100,000. Was I crazy?

Ernie called me about a week before the Breeders' Cup Race and said he had entered Ten Taylor Road in a $40,000 clamber at six furlongs. I argued with Ernie that I would not pull out of the big race just to run in a clamber. He and Pat spent two hours on the phone trying to convince me that the horse needed to enter a race he could win. I insisted I would not pull out of the big race.

The clamber was to be run on a Friday with the big race the week after on a Saturday. Ten Taylor had never run before with such a short rest. Roger and I spent endless hours on the phone discussing whether it was a good move, or not running in the clamber. What if we lost him? Would someone pay $40,000 for a 5-year old who could not beat a 78 rating and who had not run out his conditions yet? What if he ran real big in the race, could he come back so quick?

We decided to let Ernie know we would consent to run in the clamber, but if he won he would go in the big race. The clamber did not fill on Friday, Saturday or Sunday. It was held over as a special for Monday and we were entered. We could not pull out of the short field without a pretty good excuse. I called Ernie and told him that if we won we were still going in the Breeders' Cup. He brushed off my comments with one of his, "toss all right" answers.

Monday came quickly and found Ten Taylor Road 5-1 in a field which contained Mission Highland, whom we had lost to three straight times, and Downtown Clown, who could eat Mission Highland for breakfast and still be hungry for lunch. Also in the field were Good Intender, who certainly was an up and coming contender, and King Turk who used to dominate the sprints in Chicago. How was this an easy field?

Meier wanted his ride back, but Ernie gave Marquez a second ride. Meier took the ride on Downtown Clown, the favorite. Just before the race, Ernie let me give the jock instructions. I told C.H. to stick on the Clown's tail and when Randy turns around to see where he was let the horse go. I asked him to use the whip sparingly and to show the horse the stick and not hit him.

C.H. listened intently and followed my instructions perfectly. He laid off Downtown Clown by four lengths to the eighth pole and just as Randy turned to see where he was, came on like a freight train passing Meier and the tiring Clown at the wire in 1:10 3/5. We had won the race, over $13,000 in prize money and had earned a 91 Beyer rating for the race. We were ready for the Cup and a chance to beat the best in the Midwest, if we could come back in five days.

"Are you fucking out of your mind?" was all that Ernie could say in answer to my request to leave Ten Taylor in Saturday's race. Pat was less vocal...he wouldn't even talk to me. He said he had lost respect for anyone who would punish a horse by sending him back from such a hard race with only five days rest.

All that went through my mind was that we kept ducking the big races. First with supposed colic, then heat in the ankles and feet and then with an enzyme imbalance.

Now, nothing would deter me from this race. I would have to risk my animal's safety to prove his worth. The only experience I could draw on was when Ernie had put him up in place of The Ghost with only eight days rest in October and he had run big and come out all right.

I called Ernie Thursday morning, the day of the draw, and told him that if he didn't enter my horse someone else would. Ernie backed off without a whimper. However, when I asked who would be riding the horse, I found out that C.H. had taken the mount Gee Can He Dance and that Randy Meier was waiting to see if Early Fires would be in town to ride the favorite Linear, and that he wanted to stay as a backup to Fires rather than taking our ride.

We anxiously went down the list of the remaining riders and, with the exception of two apprentices, could not agree upon a rider. We were told that in a stakes race you do not get the advantage of the five pound allowance given to "bug boys." The term "bug boys" to the uninitiated might seem to infer that the jockeys are exceptionally small. In fact it applies to an apprentice jockey who gets a five-pound weight allowance for one year or until he or she has ridden their 35th winner. The five pound allowance is denoted in the program by an asterisk, or "bug" thereby creating the term "bug boy."

Ernie made a few calls and came up with David Gall. David is 52 years old and one of the leading riders in the nation. He has ridden over $2,500,000 of winners in the last two years and has been off since November. Ernie told me that David is the strongest jock he has ever met and that in the locker room the younger jockeys give him the respect and room that a king of the hill deserves. He told me that

David once rode a horse that went to its knees out of the gate and he had the strength to pull the horse upright and win the race.

The first time I met David was as he was about to mount Ten Taylor Road for the Sportsman's Budweiser Breeders' Cup Sprint. David is a year younger than me, but clothed in our colors with a riding helmet on, he looked 20 years my senior. I can only say that both Roger and I were taken aback for a moment and we giggled out of nervousness. We were five days out of a hard won contest with a 30-1 shot and a new jockey who had never ridden our horse and looked like Father Time himself.

Ernie sat in a corner of the paddock with his arms folded to let everyone know he had nothing to do with this fiasco. He could always blame it on "the fuckin' owner." He waddled up to Gall and I leaned over to make sure I heard his instructions. He told David to take the horse out but don't kill him. I then met with Gall and told him to show Ten Taylor the whip and not to hit him too often. I told him that I felt Linear and Pro Prospect were our only problems and that if we could press them we could score.

I left Ten Taylor, but not before looking into his eyes and telling him to win and returned to where Roger was standing. Roger said, "What did you tell the jock?" "I told him not to fall off!" I said.

I would eat my words. Gall rode Ten Taylor out of the gate like no one ever had. Linear and Pro Prospect joined him and soon were the leaders with De La Concord and Ten Taylor as pressers. The fractions were incredible and no one would doubt that, despite the misty rain, a track record would be set. Linear pulled away from the field exhibiting

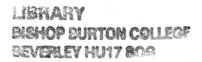

his dominance and Pro Prospect and De La Concord chased him as Ten Taylor dropped back to seventh or eighth and sought to save ground on the rail.

As I watched the track record being established by Linear at 1:08 4/5, I saw Gall and Ten Taylor Road pull off the rail to the center of the track and explode past the field for an astounding third place finish and an $11,500 share of the purse.

"I don't care if this guy is the king from the Wizard of Oz, he's our boy." I yelled at Roger, referring to Gall. We had run the three quarters in 1:09 3/5, our best time by almost a second. Someday I will be proud to tell my grandchildren that I had a horse ridden by David Gall.

I never saw Ernie after the race. Dee said he was ill and he remained silent without calling us.

I was now at a crossroads. One road sure as shooting looked like it led to failure and the other to success. Within 24 hours after our third place in the Breeders' Cup race, I received a call from Keith Miner, manager of Double D Farm in Woodstock, who offered us a breeding to Spy Signal, the most productive sire in Illinois for a mere $250 and a $10 a day board for Moonlight Drive, the mare.

I quickly made my apologies to Regal Creek Farm and Peggy and made arrangements to move Moonlight Drive to Double D for breeding. Julie was now in love with Missy's Shystar and Tim called from Horizon to say that the baby, Out for a Spin, was looking pretty good by now and might be ready to go back into training despite her parrot mouth. He gave me some hope for success. I think I have found the yellow brick road.

*"My gelding was doing pretty good until they yelled*

*they're off...he got embarrassed and crossed his legs.*"
*Buddy Hackett*

CHAPTER **21**

# CAN YOU BUY
# A RAINBOW?

After our recent success in the Breeders' Cup event I was eager to find another big race for Ten Taylor Road. The Cicero Mile was a week away. This race was another $100,000 event but was at a mile. Double T's was a proven sprinter. His experience at a mile was limited to a third place finish in the Nash as a 3-year old. I expected many of the same horses to be entered in this field as we had met two years ago, including The Ghost.

I had nominated Ten Taylor for the Cicero Mile five weeks before, tongue in cheek. Now, I was serious about running him and I awaited Ernie's reaction. I told Roger that any second now Ten Taylor would come down with some 24-hour mystery disease that would require a week's rest taking him out of the race.

I didn't even have time to hang up from that conversation when Ernie called. "Your horse is limping." he said. "We just sent him for X-rays." The story unfolded that after a morning gallop he started limping and must have either stepped on a stone or kicked himself.

The X-rays came back normal and Ernie said that all

we would need was a couple of weeks rest. Now what would you think? What am I going to do? Call Ernie a liar and put the horse in the race myself? I asked both Pat, Ernie's assistant; and Donna, his foreman, on separate occasions how the horse was doing and they supported Ernie's story. We gave the race a pass. Recoup the Cash, a sprinter like Ten Taylor, won the Cicero in 1:36 and change, and left the favorites, including The Ghost, in the dust. We had never lost to Recoup the Cash and I am certain we could have won, even at a mile.

Three days after the race, the poultice that Ten Taylor was wearing extracted a great deal of pus, thereby exonerating Ernie and making me again feel like a total asshole for doubting him. Pat was able to put Double T's shoe back on and breeze him in :50 flat for a half mile even with a pad on the sore foot. We were now ready to race again. There was a $25,000 six furlong event set for Illinois Red Letter Day. This would be a gift for us.

As luck would have it, all the other available sprinters went in a $25,000 claiming event and left us with only two competitors for the allowance which was canceled. We were now a "big horse" candidate without a big race. Our next chance to run for any decent money would be on the closing day of Sportsman's, May 7.

The Illinois Thoroughbred Breeders and Owners Foundation holds an auction once a year to sell 2-year olds in training. Many experienced buyers have been able to collar a steal in this sale and walk away with a diamond in the rough. This sale has seen a collection of crooked-legged, shin-splinted, bowed-tendoned, knock-kneed, sow-bellied, bone-chipped oat burners who sport unproven bloodline.

However, once in a while there are missed diagnoses, or breeders down to their last penny and willing to throw in a good prospect, or consignors willing to sell their entire lot of 2-year olds. The people at ITBOF had been working hard to upgrade the quality of the horses in the sale and, in general, to upgrade the quality of Illinois breeding programs. The result had been horses such as Lady Shirl coming out of the auction and attracting more and more buyers to the sale.

I looked through the auction book and carefully read the breeding of some 85 prospects. I circled the colts and geldings with early March and February foalings. I looked for black type in their breeding as well as those whose sires have been able to produce 2-year old runners. With a 2-year old filly on the farm, I didn't need to buy competition for her.

One of the most outstanding lineages belonged to Hip No. 17, a 2-year old gelding by Mari's Book, a son of Northern Dancer. He was described as a bay or dark brown and was ready to run. The only other horse that interested me was a filly by Royal Roberto.

I called Pat Devereaux and asked him if he had been over to the holding barn to see any of the sale animals. He said that he and Ernie were right on top of things and that this year's lot had several interesting horses in it. Pat mentioned his interest in Hip 17, a horse named Booker. Right away this rang a bell as I checked in my copy of the auction book and found the hip number circled in yellow with a couple of stars next to the horses name.

Pat said the horse looked like it had bilateral shin splints from mounting mares before it was gelded. He said that a type of freeze firing could cure them in no time and that this horse was well worth a look.

A call to Tim at Horizon increased my interest in Hip 17. Tim said the people at Horizon had been looking at him. He knew the boy that had been riding this youngster who said that the horse could eat up ground like a monster. Tim asked me if Ernie was going to the sale. I think Tim wanted to bid the horse for me and keep him to train. I think the world of Tim and his ability and I think we have a future together, but I can't give up on Ernie just yet. I thanked Tim for the information and called Ernie to express my intentions to bid on this horse Saturday.

Ernie told me he had heard the consignor would pull the horse out of the auction if he didn't bring at least $30,000. I told Ernie I would spend up to $20,000 for the horse. I would be up in Wisconsin for a golf tournament Saturday morning and would try to make it back in time for the auction.

I called Roger to see if he wanted any part of the purchase. Roger told me he and George Reynolds were intending to sell Just A Bonus and buy a horse together. After a lengthy conversation, Roger said if I would spend less than $15,000 on Hip 17 that he would take a third, but in no event more than $5,000. I understood Roger's position, but I was determined that even if I had to purchase the horse alone that I would. Roger also told me that he and George Reynolds were interested in bidding on the filly I had looked at.

The next day, Friday, I picked up Julie DePinto and headed out to Hawthorne to watch the 2-year olds breeze. One by one as they paraded by, I made notations in my auction book. Those that I was interested in I kept in mind by drawing a yellow circle around their number and writing in a comment. When Hip 17 breezed by, I not only noted the :10 4/5 time for the eighth of a mile as being the best of the day, but the oohs and ahhs of the crowd watching. This horse could really move. He was beautiful and athletic looking, strong and fast. I wanted this horse. I noticed two fillies with exceptional workouts also, but kept them in the back of my mind as it was a colt or gelding I really wanted.

As Murphy's law would have it again, I was held up in Wisconsin Saturday by a golf tournament that lasted longer than anticipated, and by not being able to find my wife in time to leave. Paula is a scratch shopper and can hit more stores than I can play golf holes. By the time we left Wisconsin it was after 5 p.m.

We arrived at the sales tent at Hawthorne Race Track about five minutes before the auction. If you have never been at a horse auction before, give yourself a treat, and get to one. The carnival-like activity in the tent, combined with the formalities of the sale and the parading of the animals in front of the crowd create an atmosphere of excitement usually found only at major sporting events. Everybody who was anybody in Illinois racing was there. The inner circle of buyers, trainers and agents were provided card chairs while the crowd stood roped off behind. A wooden tower held two auctioneers with an electric tote board over their heads displaying the hip number of the horse being auctioned and the last price bid.

Ernie sat in the front row, with a bright red sweater, weather-beaten black hat, and silver-tipped cane over which rested both of his gigantic hands. Dee sat at his side with Pat, Paula, myself and the ever present Dick. Ernie bent over long enough to tell me that Roger was out of my purchase and would be bidding with George Reynolds on Hip #6, the Royal Roberto filly. I told him I had brought a checkbook and would spend up to $20,000 on the gelding.

Surprisingly, the first few horses, including a Sauce Boat filly, brought anywhere from $18,000 to $30,000. Hip 6 brought a price of $7,500 paid by George and my partner Roger. Ernie winked at Pat after the purchase signifying that he had made a good buy. Evidently, the filly had a bad looking knee which everyone else took as a serious defect. Pat and Ernie felt that the problem was superficial and had nothing to do with the joint and would not affect the way she ran or her longevity.

After a few more sales, I watched as Hip 17 was led into the sales ring. My heart actually pounded when I saw him up close. He looked like a champion as he was paraded in a circle in front of the crowd. The hammer fell and the auction began. I would guess it took all of three seconds to bring the price to $21,000. Ernie, who had not flinched throughout this bidding turned to me for approval up to $25,000. I hesitated for a split second before giving a thumbs up, and as I watched Ernie's head turn back to the auctioneer to convey my bid, I saw the tote board register a bid of $28,500.

Ernie turned to me with a look of panic. "Buy the fuckin' horse, Lee, now is no time to cheap out...buy it." I hesitated for a second and gave a negative wave of my right hand as if to say I was out of the bidding. Ernie turned toward me and while looking me in the eye in the same motion nodded to the auctioneer. I watched as the tote went to $32,000, $33,500 and finally rest at $35,000. The bidding was over in a blink of an eye. My heart sank as the hammer fell at $35,000. I had not had enough time to consider whether I wanted the horse at that price or not and right now I would have paid that amount. I wanted to jump up and make another bid, even though the bidding had closed but I was interrupted by the auctioneer congratulating Ernie Poulos and myself on an excellent purchase. Ernie, still in a fixed stare in my direction, raised his cheek in a sheepish smile and winked again. "Good move," he said.

When they passed the sales slip to me for my signature, all Paula could say was, "Don't sign it. Do you realize you have just paid $35,000 for a horse that has never run?" I signed the slip, stood up, and waved good-bye at the crowd, shook a few hands and basked in my newfound warm glow of celebrity status.

The next day the racing news carried the story including the fact that Hip 17 had brought the highest price in the sale. I had either won the prize or been the jerk with the largest checkbook. In any event I owned what my trainers thought was one hell of an animal.

The next day some of the members of my country club started to syndicate a pot to purchase half of the horse. The price was to be in excess of what I had paid for the whole animal. Just as I was about to consummate the sale, Roger called me from George Reynold's bedside. George had been stricken with cancer and was under chemotherapy. "You bought a hell of a horse, partner," he said. After playing cat and mouse with Roger for over 15 minutes, a deal was struck whereby I sold them each 25 percent of Booker and took back a third of the filly for which they had paid $7,500. We agreed to keep the name Booker for the gelding but the filly was named La Royal and none of us liked the name. Since three men had purchased this female animal, it was decided to name the horse A Three Man Lady.

Tim called me from Horizon to congratulate me on the purchase and told me that although Out for a Spin was still parrot-mouthed, her hocks were much stronger and she had lost that worm belly and was looking pretty good to put back into full training. He was going to put front shoes on her and would try again to see if we could make a racing 2-year old out of her.

Meanwhile, we found a race for Ten Taylor. He had one condition left, non-winners of four other than maiden or claiming. The field contained Denouncer, Positive I.D. and the horse that had bumped him out of contention a few races ago, Simply Outstanding. The crowd leaned toward Denouncer, who had won the race in which we were bumped. Ten Taylor Road went off at 5-2. He came out of the gate well and sat on the rail a chilly third while the speed horse Positive I.D., a long shot, led around the track. At the final pole, C.H. Marquez pulled Ten Taylor off the rail to the center of the track and mounted an explosive charge to the wire which could not be answered by any of the other contestants. It was an easy win in 1:10 4/5. We were now well over $165,000 in total earnings.

On the way into the winners circle I heard a small voice yell, "nice horse Mr. Forman, how about a chance to ride him again?" The voice came from the saddle of Positive I.D.

"Nice ride E.T.," was my response. "Always glad to have you aboard."

I gave some thought to what I had said and, frankly, E.T. Baird had always been one of my favorites except for the fact that Ernie didn't get along with E.T.'s father and agent, former jockey, Bobby Baird. Bobby was one of my all-time outstanding characters in racing, and if we were not doing so well with Marquez and Gall, I would have insisted on it.

My thoughts were interrupted by the tote board flashing our number in the first place position which meant that either the stewards or some other jockey had lodged a foul claim against C.H. Marquez on our horse. My conversation with E.T. was cut short as he rode away and I turned and ran to one of the monitors to watch the replay. Sure enough, the foul claim was bullshit as the stewards and I watched for a second time as Carlos Silva ran into us with Denouncer before claiming we had cut him off. The number 2 stopped flashing and my heart stopped pounding at the same time. I was so busy at the monitor, I almost missed the win picture.

Immediately after the race I told Ernie that we would run him back on Saturday for $35,000 on the final day of racing at Sportsman's. Ernie didn't put up much of a fight this time because he knew that the race wouldn't make. Sure enough the meet ended without the six furlong event. We shipped Ten Taylor Road, Booker, and A Three Man Lady to Arlington for the start of their meet.

I visited Horizon Farm and helped shoe Out for A Spin. This was not only my first experience at assisting shoeing a horse, but it was also her first time being shoed. It took two tranquilizer shots and three of us to put on two front shoes. The experience was wonderful and the horse looked great. Her hocks were now sound and strong and she had blossomed into quite a handsome filly.

At the same time I was told that the breeding of Moonlight Drive to Spy Signal had taken and I was to be a "grandfather" again.

I met with Ernie and Dee early the next Sunday morning for coffee and doughnuts at Arlington. We mapped out a strategy for Ten Taylor Road. Since there were no short races at Arlington for big money, the horse would need to learn to go long. I asked Ernie to find a mile race and see if the horse could handle it. Both Ernie and Pat insisted that the entry of a horse in such a competitive and long race without training would be ludicrous. They both said that Ten Taylor would need several workouts both at a mile and on the turf and would have to gallop two to two and a half miles a day for at least three weeks to get ready. Roger and I agreed to take the horse off the track for the needed training and return in June for a campaign of long races. Ten Taylor Road was immediately nominated for two races for prizes of over $100,000 and the training would start with a mile workout.

That was Sunday morning. On Monday I received a call from Roger. The horse had worked a spectacular half mile and was entered in a mile race on Thursday against The Ghost and five other giants. My immediate reaction was that Ernie was having a problem finding races for Dick's horse and that he filled the race by using Ten Taylor like cannon fodder.

Ernie had selected Mark Guidry to ride Ten Taylor for the race. This was adding salt to the wound. Mark Guidry was, by far, the best rider in Chicago and will someday, in my opinion, be a Hall of Famer. However, his style of coming off the pace certainly did not fit Ten Taylor's speed and with The Ghost and Brookshire in the race we would need a rocket in the ass to catch such speed from off the pace. It looked like a great game plan for Ernie. The Ghost would be left alone on the lead to win the race and we get a nice gentle mile workout at the same time. I had seen this show before.

I called Ernie, furious at the development. I didn't want to pull the horse out of the race because both Roger and I loved the action. Even though I did not want to insult Guidry, I insisted on a jockey change and found out that C.H. had gotten homesick and returned to New York. I remembered the conversation with E.T. after the last race and insisted that he be given the mount. Ernie agreed.

The Ghost was the least of our problems. Ten Taylor had never met this class of distance runners. Double T's looked as though he could easily handle the field until the last pole when the class in the race came thundering by leaving him fourth, $2,000 richer and some 29 lengths ahead of The Ghost who had pulled up after bleeding.

One more effort at a mile was warranted and it didn't take too long to enter Ten Taylor in against some of the toughest competition that Arlington had to offer at a mile off the turf.

The result was identical. The likes of Dancing Jon, Ask Amulio and Silent Generation were sufficient to beat, but not to embarrass our sprinter. We put another $2,000 in the till but decided that it was time to return Ten Taylor to the working class and start running the sprint route again. Unfortunately for us and Ten Taylor, every time Arlington puts up a stake race or big allowance race for sprinters the same names kept popping up, Linear and Pro Prospect. Having run a route twice in a row and having trained for a longer race, Ten Taylor Road's speed was dulled and again he was forced to settle for a fourth place finish.

It is becoming painfully apparent by now that Ten Taylor Road, although having earned over $175,000 in prize money, may never be "the big horse" I have sought. We started looking around for some claiming races at six furlongs between $25,000 and $50,000. Both Roger and I have conceded that if he is taken now, that we have had a good run with him and it would better serve our interests to pay more attention to our young stock.

Just before the Fourth of July holiday, Pat Devereaux and I had a long discussion about the 2-year olds. A Three Man Lady had knocked off some spectacular workouts and we felt that since we had only paid $7,500 for her that instead of opening her up in a maiden special weight race, we would try a $25,000 maiden claiming race that would have some proven losers in it. Besides, if someone claimed her and we won, we could show quite a profit for one month of ownership.

Booker was showing blinding speed and ability on the track but was having difficulty getting used to the gate. When he broke out of the gate with other horses, he tended to shy away from them and break wide. Pat cured him of the problem by exercising him a good two miles each day before leading him to the gate. A tired horse is less likely to put up a lot of resistance at the gate. Sure enough after two or three trips like that, Booker got the idea.

Out for a Spin was getting ready to breeze for the

first time and it really appears that I may have three 2-year olds ready to race before long.

If there really is a pot of gold around, I am hoping that one of these rainbows will lead me to it.

*"As I spoke to another horseman,
the only thing I knew for sure is that
there were two dreamers in the room."*

CHAPTER **22**

# WHEN IS A DREAM
# A DREAM

I woke up with a start and peered around in the darkened
bedroom trying for a moment to separate reality from the
dream I had just experienced. Booker was going to make his
maiden start this afternoon and I had just watched the race
in my dream. I saw him break a little late from the gate and
retake the lead by the first call. I watched as he spun out of
the turn a good four lengths ahead of the field and then take
command of the race for a 10 length, hand-ridden victory. I
heard Kurt Becker's voice announcing that Booker had dec-
imated the field.

Now for the first few seconds I was trying to sort out
whether it had actually happened or I had just woken from
dreamland. What I knew was reality was that E.T. Baird had
ridden Ten Taylor Road from off the pace to easily defeat the
group of $25,000 claimers that had assembled for the
slaughter and that A Three Man Lady had run fifth in her
maiden voyage at the $25,000 level.

Right about the time you try to swallow for the first
time in the morning and it tastes like you have been chewing

on your socks all night is when reality sets in and you realize it was all just a dream. Usually prayers are said before you go to bed at night and not when you wake up, but all I remember saying before climbing in the shower that morning was, "God, let it happen that way."

I met Earl Silver at the paddock that morning and admitted to him that after all this time I was still as nervous as all hell about this race. I had 35,000 reasons for wanting the horse to perform like a champion. More importantly, as I am pursuing this dream, today might just prove to be the start of reality.

Roger and I squeezed into our tight little three-chair box to watch the race and as we saw the gate opened and out came 11 hopeful 2-year olds. The start of a maiden 2-year old race can be described only as the release of a bottle full of butterflies. Out they came, each with his own distinctive style of immaturity.

Booker, just like in the dream, had waited as the next nine horses were loaded in the gate and was caught stepping up to the gate as the bell went off. Out of the gate came the butterflies and, as I had dreamt, there was Booker on the lead by the first call. I am totally convinced that the race ran exactly as I saw it in my dream with the exception that the Daily Racing Form had him winning by only six and a half lengths. As I heard Kurt Becker's voice screaming out, "and Booker has put away this field," it seemed as though I was watching an instant replay of an old race instead of a live call.

The stands seemed to empty for the winning photograph. When Ten Taylor Road passed $180,000 in winnings only Dee and her sister Diane were in the picture. Booker, had just won a maiden special weight race and everyone and his uncle climbed into the photo. I had to push and shove my way in to get next to my own horse. Dee handed me a small goblet as a trophy presented by Allstate Insurance Company as I embraced Roger and George.

George, now a quarter partner in Booker, was just recovering from cancer surgery. He and Roger had shared a few non-winners together and, at Roger's insistence, I had let George into the deal.

George Reynolds was one of the most likable men I had ever met in my life. The first time Paula and I had met him was when we were interviewing Ernie as a trainer. Ernie had allowed George to use a small plot of land behind the barn for a garden and George was just bringing in his first crop of veggies.

I can't estimate George's age except to say that he was well into retirement. He had been a meat-counter man for Jewel Tea his whole career and had exercised his options well on Jewel stock. Upon retirement he had invested wisely and now the track and horseracing were his life. Even though George was a widower and somewhat older, I envied him quite a bit.

On the occasion of our first meeting he was dressed in his gardening jeans and was filthy. Paula handed him some gum wrappers for disposal as if he were some barn help. George, true to his nature, accepted the garbage and with a smile and a nod, disposed of it. I do not know if Paula ever got over being embarrassed after learning his true identity. "How did I know? Look how he was dressed," was her constant answer whenever confronted with the event.

George had brought two relatives to the race and as I was introduced to them, I shook their hands and gave

George a little hug. George had survived the cancer surgery and was now taking radiation. The win was the best medicine that money could buy.

I watched videos of the race that evening. I know that this must be the first time anyone ever videotaped a dream.

By the end of the month, Ten Taylor Road was ready to run again. Being afraid of losing him in a small claiming race, we entered him in a $35,000 claimer at six and a half furlongs. A Kentucky horse by the name of Soar on Wings was the favorite of the seven sprinters that entered the gate that day. E.T. was wearing our brand new silks which button down the middle and provided more room for the flak jackets the jocks were now all required to wear. A black tie was added to give just a little bit of class to the uniform.

Soar on Wings was no challenge for the off-the-pace charge that Ten Taylor put on that afternoon. It only took 1:17 for Double T's to put away this field of claimers. We had now won three in a row. Our earnings so far for the month of July exceeded $32,000.

We had a decision to make in the case of Booker. Ernie and Pat felt we should pick out a nice soft non-winners of two race and let him destroy another field. Roger and I wanted him to go up against the big kids on the block to see what we had.

Our power struggle with Ernie had entered another phase. Ernie was being bothered again by his diabetes and was not spending as much time as usual in the barn. Pat was slowly taking over all of the training decisions and Dee was running the business. Ernie made as many token appearances as he could and would not admit that he was sick but the truth was painfully apparent.

Dick had lost his power struggle with Ernie and pulled all of his horses out of the barn and left for another trainer. Dick felt that at $45 a day per horse that he could expense out his stable at a lower cost by buying a full-time trainer and paying all the costs. Only time will tell if he is correct or not.

Dick's departure left me with two of the three big horses in the barn. Ernie was not about to pick a fight with either Roger or me. Booker was entered in the $50,000 Chicago Juvenile against horses shipped in by D. Wayne Lukas and Dogwood Stables. These puppies were being primed to go for the gold. Ernie and Pat were afraid Booker would shy in the presence of such horses and would set himself back.

Pat and I had an hour long discussion on the subject and I was informed, as I had never realized before, that horses can intimidate other horses in the paddock area. Much like one horse is the leader in the wild, a horse can attempt to intimidate another horse with some type of conduct that creates a fear in the attacked horse, not to take the lead on the attacker.

Pat, by this time, had pretty much taken over the daily operations for Ernie who was becoming more and more seriously ill. Pat had come from four generations of horsemen and had devoted his life to the industry. Pat is sort of a roly poly little guy whose weight fluctuates with the season. He had an uncanny ability to lose tons of weight and then eat himself back into trouble. Notwithstanding his only bad habit of eating, this was a man who understood animals. More and more his genius and experience with the

Thoroughbred was exhibited.

Pat seemed to honor Ernie's experience and like the other employees referred to him with a reverent "Boss." Pat stayed clear of me for quite some time and our relationship grew out of my increased trust in his decisions. Pat kept saying, "I'm not going to say anything one way or another to you Mr. Forman, because you are going to do what you want to do anyway." I learned how to glean information from him and then make decisions based on his experience.

Pat explained to me that Booker was, at the present time, a coward. His speed might be attributable to his having to run away from danger just as the hero did in the movie "Forrest Gump." The horses entered in the Juvenile might all be leaders of the pack and subject our poor little Booker to tremendous intimidation.

I didn't buy the argument fully and Booker would run in the Juvenile, a six furlong event.

The day of the race found me a disaster area as I didn't sleep a wink the night before. Spencer and Melissa, my son and daughter, had invited their crowd, and Paula and I had invited half the neighborhood. Booker had pulled post 8 in the eighth race which was my lucky race and post position. The jockey was sporting our new silks with crossed gavels and an eight ball.

The track record for five furlongs at Arlington had held since 1970 at :57 1/5. Just :57 3/5 after the start of the race we stood motionless as Booker passed the five furlong mark in the lead. But then, just as Ernie and Pat had feared, the pack of intimidating wolves began to bark at our frightened little puppy and he stopped running. We ran ninth of eleven. Booker, without a sweat, jogged back to the paddock, still looking around like a child on his first trip to Disney World. Neither the experience of E.T. nor the blinkers he wore could quell his fears or curiosity.

We walked away, not only empty-handed, but with a little sick feeling that comes from the confusion of not knowing whether this would be a minor setback or a pattern. As Marty McGee, the Illinois correspondent of the Daily Racing Form, had put it the day before the big race, "All the owners in this race have nothing but high hopes. Will they be dashed or justified?"

Pat and I had a chance to chew the fat about the race three days later. I still loved to visit the barn early in the morning and watch the workouts and the activities that morning brought. My main effort was trying to blend into the background and try not to get in anyone's way.

I knew what Pat was thinking before he said it. He never would have run Booker in that open race so soon. He wanted Booker to gain maturity, confidence and knowledge as to what this whole game is about before throwing him up against the best that open racing can offer. What he said made sense. After all, I kept complaining that Ten Taylor Road was excluded from all of the Illinois races, why not take advantage of the other side of the coin with Booker?

Booker would go back into training by running with tougher, older horses and would learn to shake his fears.

This would be a month of mistakes. After winning three in a row, my head had swelled to the size of a watermelon. First I would throw Booker to the wolves and now I entered Ten Taylor in an allowance race that was so far over his head that it embarrasses me to chronicle the results other than to say that it was only the second time in 42 races he failed to bring home a check.

E.T. eased the horse to save him and after the leaders crossed the finish line, they had to send out a search party for my black beauty. Nothing teaches a lesson better than losing. No one ever gained knowledge from a win. Horses, like people, find their place in life, and Ten Taylor was not destined to be my "big horse." He would become a hardknocker, running in claimers until that eventuality which would retire him.

Booker would now carry my hopes and dreams.

By now Ernie had gone through what we all thought would be some minor surgery and had taken some extended time away from the barn. Most all of my race planning was now with Pat, which was to my liking. I enjoyed the company of Pat and Dee. I had mixed feelings about the future but for now I was satisfied.

Booker would run in a non-winners of two races, for Illinois-breds only. If he could beat that group it would leave races such as the Signor Cotton and Chief Illiniwek as easy picking. I had a lump in my throat with the knowledge that we would forego the Arlington Futurity and the Arch Ward. Those major stake races usually launch the winners into fame and fortune. Our plan was to have Booker beat up on his own kind first before going into open company.

The day of the race found me in another golf tournament. It was our annual club championship and I was only one stroke off the lead after seven holes. I looked at my watch and walked off the course. This will give you an idea of where my priorities were at the time.

I watched as Pat put the tack on Booker and I was disappointed to see that our new gold and black checkered blinkers were not ready yet. The old blue blinkers, however, had a new diamond-shaped hole in them so that Booker could catch sight of any horse which made a run at him. We hoped that this would solve the problem of him stopping.

As long as I have been watching racing, I have never seen a horse leave a gate as fast as Booker did that day. He stayed about two lengths in front of the pack pacing himself for the last furlong. At the five furlong mark, two horses, Venus in Spurs and Slight Prospect made a move on Booker and for a fraction of a second it looked like a repeat of the stakes race. Booker started losing ground to the oncoming horses and then, as E.T. changed to a left handed whip, Booker changed leads and held off the challengers by a good three quarters of a length. We had recouped two-thirds of his purchase price with this win and were now ready for an Illinois-bred handicap.

As Booker was led back into the winners circle, he balked at the two pots of roses swinging in the wind. This puppy was afraid of anything that moved. Notwithstanding that fact, as I took the photo that day something told me that, indeed, I may have found a final chapter to this book. What an irony to have the final chapter of a book written about a horse named Booker.

My involvement in the racing game was increasing in direct proportion to the number of horses I had actively racing. I was now looking forward to a Labor Day weekend of three racing days in a row. First, A Three Man Lady would try to break her maiden. Ten Taylor Road would again drop into the claiming ranks, followed by a try at a stakes win by Booker in the Signor Cotton Handicap. At the same time I was looking forward to Out for A Spin to go back into training and get ready for Hawthorne.

The day before the first of the three races, I was so sure that all three would win, that I a made a three horse parlay bet with an OTB teller, betting A Three Man Lady to win and asking him to bet all the winnings on Ten Taylor Road and, if he won, the entire pot on Booker.

A Three Man Lady really looked ready for her attempt at breaking her maiden. She pulled the number 5 slot in a field of 12. The event was at six furlongs and we still were not sure if that was long enough for her specific talents. Mark Guidry, who was the perfect jockey for this filly, would again get the ride and this time would attempt to come from off the pace.

When the bell went off, "Lady" got a pretty good start. However, this time, Mark settled her down to running at a nice even pace. I felt she was too far off the pace when Mark retreated to the back of the pack in Guidry style. Our colors were not even in the TV screen when the horses turned for home. Then I saw Lady beginning her attack by weaving through the traffic and at the eighth pole she changed leads and began an assault on the leaders. The field looked as it was standing still as A Three Man Lady charged past the pack to win and break her maiden in classic Guidry style.

Roger, George and I were again joined by a throng in the winners circle. Pat had a smile on his face from ear to ear and was shouting over and over "Wait until the Debutante!" I knew he meant the $100,000 race for Illinois 2-year old fillies at the beginning of October. I also noticed, for the first time, that Ernie had not joined us in the winners circle. He had not done so for at least the last four races.

Ernie was content to sit in the paddock and watch the race on a TV monitor. Ernie was not well enough to keep making the trip to the winners circle because of his diabetes, the minor surgery he had gone through, and the condition of his knees.

The joy of victory was saddened the very next day. Not only did Ten Taylor Road lose the six furlong claimer, but he was claimed from the race. E.T. had gotten Ten Taylor strung out 10 horses wide and the best that he could do from there was fifth. A trainer from Louisiana, named Louis Roussel III, had claimed him for $25,000. He planned to take him down to the Fair Grounds in La. for the winter. The new owners were good people and would take good care of the horse. In fact, Roger asked the new trainer if he would sell us back the horse at a small profit and he agreed. However, in conference with Pat, Roger and George, we decided that spending $25,000 on a 5-year old who would get no better than he was and could not beat open company was not wise. I only asked the trainer for his halter for my collection and spent a few final seconds in the detention barn with the horse who might have been my "big horse" before leaving him for the last time. I had learned my lesson well from my experiences with Motion Call. I will never fall in love with an animal again.

It seemed only a short time had passed before they loaded Booker in the gate for the Signor Cotton Handicap. My heart was pounding in my chest. Beating this small group of animals would ensure us as favorites in at least the next three big races. My goal was establishing domination over these Illinois-breds and gaining status. As the bell went off, we were a strong second favorite.

I could not find my colors among the leaders at the first call so I directed my attention back to the gate where, in horror, I saw Booker on his belly. The ground in front of him had given way under his first leaping assault. His front legs buckled and he crumpled to the ground striking his mouth and chest. E.T. stayed with him and raised him up and began a slow gallop to evaluate the damage. The field began to distance him when E.T. had him back at full speed. At first it appeared that the impossible was about to happen. One by one Booker caught the field only to fall short by a mere five lengths. There is good and bad in every happening. The good part is that even though he had fallen and had bled in a sprint race, he was capable of catching a very strong field to finish fourth only a few lengths off the leader. Booker had proven that he had a ton of heart.

As we took the long march through the tunnel back to the paddock, Pat began mumbling. He was saying over and over again, "That's the last time." I asked him what he meant and he said, "That's the last fucking time we get cheated out of a win by Lady Luck." "Let bad luck visit someone else for a change."

It didn't take "Lady Luck" very long to answer Pat's call. As summer gave way to fall we entered Booker in the $50,000 Chief Illiniwek named in honor of the mascot of the University of Illinois football team. This race would again match us up against Venus in Spurs and Attivo in a field of 10 horses.

With my wife and I and both our children alumni of the U of I it seemed destined that this would be an ideal place for Booker to enter the ranks of stakes winners.

The day was perfect. The sun was shining brightly,

the stands were full, and Paula and I were surrounded by several of our close friends as well as Dawn, Roger and George, our partners. Booker was unusually uncomfortable with his tongue tie in the paddock, and most of the trainers had their hands full just keeping their 2-year olds in tow.

Everything seemed just right. Well, almost every-thing. "Lady Luck" was being a shit again. E.T. Baird, the only jock who had ever ridden Booker, was given a five-day suspension just three days before and we just learned that only stake races over $75,000 are exceptions to such a sus-pension. In other words we would have to search for another jockey just before the race. Eusebio (Eddie) Razo Jr. took the ride and favored us with a conference with E.T. just before the race. Next, Booker had pulled the same seven post he had fallen in during the last disaster. All of the handicappers had made Venus in Spurs the favorite with the exception of "Sweeps." At race time we were 2-1 with Venus at 8-5.

For the first time, Booker entered the gate like a pro and stood silently and patiently awaiting the starting bell. I truly do not remember whether I was standing or sitting or whether I kept bouncing up and down before the start of the race, but the adrenaline was flowing. It was like watching an instant replay of a race for the first time, that you would watch over and over later, trying to will the ending to be in your favor. For some dumb reason I kept thinking of the sick gambler who lost $300 on the race and $250 on the replay. However, that is truly how you feel at a time like this. When you know this moment may be replayed over and over in the future you treat the actual moment as a replay.

Booker came out at a slower pace about a length off the lead. Like a good young professional who is learning his trade he did not make the same mistake twice. After grabbing the track he was able to take the lead at the first call. From that point until the three eighths pole, he led the field by two to three lengths with easy long strides that seemed to mock the efforts of those chasing him. Booker was not yet the kind of horse who is just content to beat the other horses in a race. Booker was still a green youngster and treated every race like playtime in the field. Taunting the field he turned his head back and slowed down to challenge anyone who would dare to race him. Venus, with Guidry aboard, answered the call and came on with vengeance. Booker was caught at the half mile mark. Guidry, the master of off the pace, was advancing with every stride and as he and his mount came head to head, Eddie Razo went to the whip and Booker went to work. Off he went to a full length and a half lead. You would have thought play time was over. No. Have you ever seen a pro football player at the end of a touchdown run back into the end zone while pointing at the tiring defense sprawled before him? Booker must have seen one of those games because before the finish line, he seemingly stopped and walked across the line as the ever-trying Venus in Spurs answered the mockery with a late burst of unbelievable speed. The result was a head bobbing photo finish.

Watching the photo sign go black and the board light up with a big number seven was a moment I shall not forget. The winner's circle picture, the champagne toast and the back slapping and hand shaking, the waving to friends in the stands are all a blur. I had once looked at the owners in the paddock surrounded by a gaggle of reporters and television cameras and wished that I could be them. Well, no sooner had the bulbs stopped flashing, I was whisked away and found myself staring into the barrel of a .45 caliber TV camera with a microphone stuffed up my nose and fielding questions I was ill-prepared to answer. My mouth was moving and sound was coming out of it as I could hear my words echo through the walls of Arlington Park. Thousands of strangers hung on my every utterance and my likeness was being broadcast on several screens the size of drive-in theaters.

As I spoke I could envision Lou Gehrig as his words bounced around Yankee stadium...I consider...er er er myself the luckiest, est est est man on the face, face face, of the earth th th th. Fortunately, I had the good sense not to mock one of the most memorable speeches in the history of sports, but at last I had a small taste of the dream. The words of Pat Devereaux now ran through my mind. "I think you have bought yourself an ending to your book."

*"There is only one thing that bothers me about my
memory of races and I can't remember what that is."*

CHAPTER **23**

# IN HOT PURSUIT...
# THE GOAL IS NEAR

As far as I can remember, I have not missed a single race of any horse I have owned. At worst I have watched one or two on closed circuit TV from an OTB. Paula and I had planned a two week trip to Greece to celebrate her birthday and I would miss the Don Leon Stakes and Booker's second attempt at open company as well as A Three Man Lady's run at $25,000 platers.

Both Toy Boy and Out for A Spin, my 2-year olds that had not yet raced, were in training at Hawthorne Race Course and it was my hope that we could get a race out of each of them before the season ended. Everywhere I went people asked me about Ten Taylor Road and why I had not attempted to buy him back. I had justified my decision to myself and I was not about to change my mind. However, a certain bet I had made came back to haunt me.

My good friend Everett Ellin and I had made a bet almost a year ago and neither of us had contemplated Ten Taylor Road being claimed. I had bet Everett $500 that Ten Taylor Road could earn $200,000 in purse money between Thanksgiving 1993 and Memorial Day 1995. Up to the day that he was claimed in he had touched the $75,000 mark for that time period, with total lifetime earnings just a tad under $200,000. Without control of what races he would be in, it would be impossible for me to control the bet and I felt the bet should have been called off at that point.

Everett and I got together over a cup of coffee and I decided that in order to complete the bet I had to buy half the horse back from Roussel. Everett and I then altered the bet. He would receive 1 percent of my winnings until Memorial Day 1995 in consideration of the bet and, if the horse did indeed go over $200,000 in earnings, he would return all that I had paid him.

I called Roussel, who was as much of a gentleman as I had heard, and he accepted half the price he had paid and half the costs he had incurred since the purchase in exchange for an equal interest in Ten Taylor Road. The horse would run as soon as the Fair Grounds opened in late November.

We were some 100 miles off the coast of Rhodes, Greece, and in the middle of a jet black sea with bolts of lightning and swells of ten feet or more pitching our vessel to and fro when I made a $150 ship to shore call to get the replay of Booker's near win of the Don Leon Stakes. Booker had given up eight pounds to the open field as he carried 122 pounds in the stakes, his first attempt beyond three quarters of a mile. The extra weight, length of the race and open company kept him just shy of victory as Koennecker, a Lou Goldfine-trained colt, by Arts and Letters took the win.

A second, equally expensive, phone call the next day produced a little better result. A Three Man Lady, guided by Mark Guidry, had come from 20 lengths off the pace to score a seven and a half length victory over 25,000 platers.

This would be the first photo I would hang without being in the picture.

Each year, the Illinois Thoroughbred Breeders and Owners Association recognizes certain horses for their accomplishments the preceding year. One of the awards is for the "Champion Illinois Two-Year Old Colt or Gelding of the Year." This award would be significant enough to recognize the winner as a "big horse." Booker was the leading candidate for this prize. Only Venus in Spurs, Ballyneety Saint and possibly Attivo were in contention.

My plan now was to run Booker in the Illinois Cavalier Stakes the day after Thanksgiving and if the weather permitted, to run him in the Bold Bidder Stakes a week before Christmas. This would allow him to prove himself as the best Illinois-bred 2-year old and still give us enough time to rest him over the winter and train him long for his 3-year old campaign. We would let a Three Man Lady have another crack at a stakes win in the Silent Beauty and attempt to pay for the long cold winter with Ten Taylor Road running down at the Fair Grounds in New Orleans.

November 5 brought the Breeders' Cup from Kentucky. To a horseplayer this day is the World Series, Super Bowl and Stanley Cup all rolled into one. The dreams of hitting the pick seven on November 5 transcend the possibility of eternal life.

As each of the owners approached the paddock to receive that small statute which represented a Breeders' Cup victory, I swallowed hard trying to imagine what it would be like.

I remembered the day I received the Breeders' Cup trophy for Double T's win in the Lost Code and my recent

TV interview after Booker's triumph in the Illiniwek and tried to imagine what those experiences would be like multiplied by 10.

For only the second time in history (the first being Ernie's victory with Black Tie Affair) a Chicago-based horse won a Breeders' Cup Race. Most notably the horse's name was One Dreamer, a filly trained by Tommy Proctor. I cried as I watched Tommy's assistant trainer, running behind the winner as she was paraded past the grandstands, holding on to her tail with his left hand and tipping his hat to the crowd with his right hand as he bowed to the waist with his graying pony tail waiving in the wind. Tears rolled down his cheeks and I imagined he was trying hard to preserve the moment forever.

I know Ernie had felt the same way right after Black Tie Affair had won, and I longed for that feeling, that incredible feeling of ecstasy, exhilaration and accomplishment all wrapped into one that would justify the expense, the heartbreak, the agony of defeat, and the patience that the sport required. I would know my goals had been attained when I tasted that feeling.

When we returned from Greece I found out just how expensive satellite phone calls were. The bill was just over $850. That will be the last time I bounce anything off anything else.

A Three Man Lady was entered in the Silent Beauty Stakes with 13 other hopefuls. One of the horses was a filly called Doc's Delimma who had won her maiden race by 7 lengths, running an astounding 1:10 4/5 for six furlongs. This type of speed was almost unheard of in a 2-year old Illinois-bred filly.

A Three Man Lady was the third favorite at 9-1 behind the 3-5 speedball. Guidry broke her alertly out of the gate and settled in about seventh place along the rail and allowed the speed horses to challenge the favorite. Nothing could catch or press Doc's Delimma that day. She would have her way as the uncontested speed. The remainder of the field, exhausted by the chase, began to fall by the wayside, making them easy pickings for our fast finishing filly. We lost by a good seven lengths, but a second behind this kind of filly was as good as a win. We had beaten almost all of the contenders for top Illinois-bred with the exception of the horse which I am sure will be named the champ.

The win added another $10,500 to her winnings bringing A Three Man Lady over the $30,000 mark as her 2-year old season drew to a close. She was still eligible to run in an Illinois only, non-winners of a race as her only two victories came at the expense of $25,000 claimers. If the race would go we could easily add another photo to the album. Booker had surpassed the $70,000 mark in his young career. Our investment folly for a sum total of $42,500 had more than doubled in prize money in the first six months.

Louie called me from the Fair Grounds and told me that Ten Taylor Road was working beautifully and that he expected to run him at six furlongs on November 26 in a claimer for $32,500. That would be the same day Booker would run in a race that might determine championship honors. This might prove to be the red letter day I had been waiting for. It might not be The Breeders' Cup Classic, or the Kentucky Derby, but to me, it would mark my graduation into the ranks of those I have envied from afar.

Just prior to the Thanksgiving weekend races, I had

an opportunity to recap my entire record up to this date as an owner. Our Tsunami Su had run nine times with one win two seconds, one third, and had earned $13,004. Ten Taylor Road had run thirty-nine times with nine wins, seven seconds, ten thirds, and had only missed three checks by running worse than fifth a mere 3 times and brought home just slightly under $200,000 in earnings. A Three Man Lady had run seven times with a record of two, one and one for $29,866 and Booker was in the winners circle in half of his six races, had one second, and was just over the $69,000 mark.

The horses that I had owned in part or whole had run 61 times and, not counting the time that Ten Taylor's number was taken down, had won an astounding 15 races or just a hair under 25 percent of the time. My little puppies had been in the money 62 percent of the time and had brought home the bacon by being in the top five in 89 percent of their races. They had run and returned an average of just under $5,000 per race with a total earnings of over $300,000.

As the racing season of 1994 drew to a close and my goal of owning of a "big horse" came closer and closer, I became more in tune with both the sport and business of racing. Baseball and hockey were now on strike and this year would go down in history with only an asterisk where the World Series should have been, and the opening of the new United Center in Chicago would happen without a single punch being thrown.

Dick Duchossois had threatened not to open Arlington if the state legislature did not give him a right to operate casino gambling and if it were not for the intervention of Tom Carey and Stormy Bidwill we might not have had a 1995 season at Arlington. The two other track owners agreed to split the losses of Arlington and Dick agreed to a 55 day racing schedule instead of the usual 130 days.

The jockeys were poised to go on strike the first of the year if the tracks did not contribute one cent out of every $10 bet to their pension and health plan.

On the local scene, some of the finest trainers of all time had been either suspended or fined for supposed use of an illegal drug, and Ernie was back in the hospital to have his gall bladder removed. Troy Patrick had died and my partner George Reynolds had totally recovered from his cancer. Roger, Paula, Dawn and I had gained a combined 100 pounds over the period; and our cat Frisky, who had used up 12 of her nine lives when this book started, finally used them all up.

Ernie's ex-groom Teri is still alive; Dee, his wife, hasn't changed an iota. Mark Guidry, Randall Meier and E.T. Baird are the three leading jocks at the present meet and the same guys show up day after day at the OTBs.

Motion Call has probably been rendered by now and Missy's Shystar is still so obstinate, Julie hasn't been able to ride her yet. Moonlight Drive is as fat as a pig and will probably deliver us a foal by Spy Signal in February. Our Tsunami Su is still the favorite pet of a little blind girl in eastern Wisconsin.

This Thanksgiving Day weekend would either reward me with the victory that would propel Booker into the limelight as a "big horse" or would tease me in my search for that elusive "15 minutes of fame" that everyone supposedly gets. I had hoped to start off the weekend with a victory out of A Three Man Lady, sandwich it with the needed win out of Booker and cap it off with a win out of Ten Taylor Road at the Fair Grounds.

A Three Man Lady could only provide me with a check for $1,800 as Guidry could not catch the uncontested cheap speed of a filly who probably will never win another race in her entire career. Fortunately, my filly returned healthy and would go on several weeks later to cap off her 2-year old season with an allowance win, bringing her 1994 winnings to just under $45,000.

As Booker was being loaded into the number 2 stall, all I could think of were the events over the past three years. The education I had gained, my experiences with Ernie, Dee, Teri, Roger, Pat, E.T., and all the marvelous characters I have had the good fortune to meet during this time. I was shaking as the adrenaline flowed. The entire experience could be capped by a win in this race.

Exclusive Garth had been sidelined by a fracture, Attivo was likewise history as a result of an injury. Venus in Spurs had been given the rest of the season off and only three horses—Incognito, Ballyneety Saint and possibly Puff of Carb—could match the speed and stamina of Booker. Eddie Razo, who had won the Chief Illiniwek riding Booker, was aboard Incognito and would make a run at the finish, and Ray Sibille was on Ballyneety Saint and would certainly challenge and press Booker all the way.

I had instructed E.T. to make certain Booker did not bolt from the gate and take a chance on falling as he had before and also reminded him to keep the horse's mind on the race the whole way. E.T. sensed the importance of the race and listened intently to my instructions. He had also picked up another five-day suspension for interfering with another jockey during a November 23 race and had gained a stay of the suspension to ride in this race.

As Paula buried her head under her arms and turned the bell went off. Booker came out safely and steadily went to the lead as Ballyneety Saint took second as a presser. Razo kept Incognito close, saving something for a final run at us.

Booker led throughout the race, as the relative positions of the horses did not change. The slow fractions seemed to indicate that Incognito, off the pace by five or six lengths, would not have a run at either Ballyneety Saint or Booker. As the horses passed the eighth pole, Booker led by half a length as he and Ballyneety Saint made it look like a two horse race. All I could think of was that there was only one horse between me and my goal.

With barely 25 yards to go I watched in horror as Ballyneety Saint caught Booker and grabbed a full head lead. I felt we were beaten, without a doubt. The horses had not yet crossed the line as I swallowed hard, blinked and tried to erase from my sight Ballyneety Saint pulling away from Booker with just a few feet to go. All my hopes, my dreams and my quest for a "big horse" were inches away from disappointment.

But Booker, peeking out of the diamond shaped opening in the blinkers that he wore, caught sight of Ballyneety Saint and responded to a left-handed crack of the whip by E.T. Booker's stride lengthened and his thick young supple neck stretched out. The last of his three or four desperate grabs of ground propelled him nose to nose with Ballyneety as they crossed the line. The photo sign lit up brightly. The crowd's roar quieted to a whisper and not a breath was taken as all eyes stared intently on the replay of the race and on the tote board.

Paula turned to me and asked if we had won or lost. I did not respond. I just pointed to the tote board as it displayed a brightly lit number 2 in the first position followed by an 8. Booker's heart and his determination to win, commodities you cannot feel or see when you buy a horse, had propelled him to victory.

After three years of cultivating Ten Taylor Road as my standard-bearer, and after hoping that Motion Call would win the big race and rise up on his hind legs like Trigger, and after giving away two fillies, along comes Booker—and from Easter to Thanksgiving justifies all the expense and time I have spent in this game.

As our groom, Ruben Mata, led Booker out of the winners circle and back to the barn, he turned to me, gave me a thumbs up sign and a wink, and started shouting in broken Spanish, "Out of da way...big horse a comin'."

The tears of joy had hardly dried from my face when we arrived at Arlington Track Side Restaurant to watch the satellite broadcast of Ten Taylor Road's first race at the Fair Grounds. One minute and 10 seconds after the race had started, Paula and I watched our second win of the day as Ten Taylor Road resurrected himself as a candidate for a "big horse" by whipping the best that the Fair Grounds could throw at him.

I will celebrate my 54th birthday in a few days. When I am long gone, my great-grandchildren can open up the scrapbook that Paula and I have kept, and leaf through the newspaper articles, photos, autographs and memorabilia that I have collected during the past three years, and will continue to collect until my dying day, and see what I had accomplished. Somewhere there will be a book which will bear my name and the names of the horses that have won stakes races for me. I have done little to change the history of the world, but I have set out to accomplish a goal and have, at least in my own eyes, succeeded.

For all of you who dream that someday you can reach your goals, my only words of encouragement are that you can do whatever you set out to do. There is no star that is out of reach.

Now when I hear Ernie's first words echo in my mind, "So you wanna own fuckin' horses, huh?" I answer over and over again to myself, "Yeah, no questions asked, I wanna own fuckin' horses."

**Our Tsunami Su**   12/5/91   Hawthorne   First win for Samson & Forman Stables
Pictured from left to right: Lee Forman, Paula Forman, Dawn Samson, Roger Samson, Ernie Poulos, Donna Pilipiak (stable foreman), Mark Guidry (jockey), Charlie Bettis

**Ten Taylor Road** 3/21/94 Sportsman's Park
Pictured from left to right: Pat Deveraux (asst. trainer), Dee Poulos, Roger Samson, Lee Forman, Rubin Mata (groom), C.H. Marquez Jr.

**Booker**   The Chief Illiniwek Stakes   9/21/94   Arlington International
Pictured from left to right: George Reynolds, Ben Samson, Paula Forman, Dr. Everett Ellin (in background), Lee Forman, Rubin Mata, Eusebio Razo Jr. (jockey)

**A Three Man Lady** 12/15/94 Hawthorne
Pictured from left to right: Susan O'Hare, Mary Eddington (L. P. Forman's legal secretaries), Spencer Forman, Roger Samson, Dawn Samson, Ben Samson, 2 unidentified grooms, Mark Guidry (jockey)

**Booker**   Illinois Cavalier Stakes   11/26/94   Hawthorne
Pictured left to right: Dawn Samson & son Ben, Roger Samson, Paula Forman, Lee Forman, Mike Corn, George Reynolds, Bobbie Baird (in background), Rubin Mata, E.T. Baird (jockey)

**Booker**   Illinois Cavalier Stakes   11/26/94   Hawthorne
(also pictured number 8 Ballyneety Saint) photo finish